HowExpert
Balle

C000133931

101+ Tips to Learn How to Get Started in Ballet, Discover Tips & Tricks, and Become a Better Ballet Dancer

HowExpert with Lauren Dillon

Copyright HowExpert™
www.HowExpert.com

For more tips related to this topic, visit HowExpert.com/ballet.

Recommended Resources

- HowExpert.com – Quick 'How To' Guides on All Topics from A to Z by Everyday Experts.
- HowExpert.com/free – Free HowExpert Email Newsletter.
- HowExpert.com/books – HowExpert Books
- HowExpert.com/courses – HowExpert Courses
- HowExpert.com/clothing – HowExpert Clothing
- HowExpert.com/membership – HowExpert Membership Site
- HowExpert.com/affiliates – HowExpert Affiliate Program
- HowExpert.com/jobs – HowExpert Jobs
- HowExpert.com/writers – Write About Your #1 Passion/Knowledge/Expertise & Become a HowExpert Author.
- HowExpert.com/resources – Additional HowExpert Recommended Resources
- YouTube.com/HowExpert – Subscribe to HowExpert YouTube.
- Instagram.com/HowExpert – Follow HowExpert on Instagram.
- Facebook.com/HowExpert – Follow HowExpert on Facebook.
- TikTok.com/@HowExpert – Follow HowExpert on TikTok.

Publisher's Foreword

Dear HowExpert Reader,

HowExpert publishes quick 'how to' guides on all topics from A to Z by everyday experts.

At HowExpert, our mission is to discover, empower, and maximize everyday people's talents to ultimately make a positive impact in the world for all topics from A to Z...one everyday expert at a time!

All of our HowExpert guides are written by everyday people just like you and me, who have a passion, knowledge, and expertise for a specific topic.

We take great pride in selecting everyday experts who have a passion, real-life experience in a topic, and excellent writing skills to teach you about the topic you are also passionate about and eager to learn.

We hope you get a lot of value from our HowExpert guides, and it can make a positive impact on your life in some way. All of our readers, including you, help us continue living our mission of positively impacting the world for all spheres of influences from A to Z.

If you enjoyed one of our HowExpert guides, then please take a moment to send us your feedback from wherever you got this book.

Thank you, and we wish you all the best in all aspects of life.

Sincerely,

BJ Min
Founder & Publisher of HowExpert
HowExpert.com

PS...If you are also interested in becoming a HowExpert author, then please visit our website at HowExpert.com/writers. Thank you & again, all the best!

Table of Contents

Author's Foreword

This guide has been created for anyone considering starting ballet classes, has a child who dances, or wants to know a little more about the dance style. This book has been designed to guide you through the beginning stages of your ballet journey.

Ballet has been something that has shaped me into the person I am today. Ballet has taught me that if you want something, you must work as hard and for as long as it takes to reach your goals. That it's okay to fall, need help, and be wrong sometimes. It has taught me time management, preparedness, respect, and to love something so deeply that it becomes a part of you.

While I am not a professional ballet dancer, I have been dancing for over two decades. I have been a ballet teacher off and on for several years. I have worked with dance archival material and written about dance. I do not consider myself to know everything there is to know about ballet. It is impossible to know everything. This book, however, discusses subjects that I have years of experience in and feel are relevant to you, the reader.

"Ballet is a dance executed by the human soul." Alexander Pushkin.

Chapter 1: Finding the Best Studio for You

The first step in starting your ballet journey is to find a studio where you can take classes. Unfortunately, not all studios are created equally, and it is essential to do a little research before your first class. Your ballet goals and need should be considered when choosing a dance studio.

Tip 1: A Google Search is a Good Way to Start.

While it seems like Googling "Ballet Studio Near Me" is an obvious starting point, it will be the best for finding local studios. Reading reviews can be a helpful thing. It is a bit easier for children to find a studio because most studios teach kids from ages 3 to 18. The only thing you should be looking for in studios for your child is if they teach solid technique. The proper technique is vital in learning to dance. Your child will also benefit from the structured rules in a technique-based class. The teachers have been teaching children of all ages and know what each class level needs and the skills to develop.

A Boutique Studio is an excellent option if you want to do Mommy/Daddy and Me classes. Or creative movement classes with a very young child. Creative movement is a class structured around moving in different ways. For example, crawling, hopping, and walking on the tips of their toes. There also is an element of musicality that is focused on as well. Free dancing to music or dancing while pretending to be a butterfly is great for a young child. It is a form of imaginative play that helps with balance and movement skills, and the kids love it.

Tip 2: Adult classes are not as easy to find, but they are out there

After deciding to take the plunge and take a ballet class, the search for a studio to go to can sometimes be a bit of a challenge. Many studios do not offer adult classes but don't let this discourage you. You may have to dig into a website to see if there is a Beginning or

Intro to Ballet class for adults. Professional ballet companies will be the first place to look. The class times and schedules vary the most at a professional company. It helps to write down the studio's class schedule for adults when you find a few different places to take classes. Once you find a studio or studios, all that is left to consider is fitting ballet classes into your schedule.

Many adult classes are offered in the evenings. Instructors know you may be coming to the studio straight from work. Evenings tend to work better for almost all adult students. It isn't uncommon to see courses scheduled at 10 am or noon for classes at professional ballet companies. Your teachers are active dancers and teach classes before or after their rehearsals. If you can attend these morning/afternoon classes, that is great. If you can't, it's not the end of the world. You also may want to look up or ask about the frequency of adult classes offered at a studio. Some adult dancers are comfortable with taking one class a week. Still, others will take more than one beginner class a week because they enjoy taking classes. It doesn't matter how many classes you take as an adult per week. Taking class consistently is what is essential.

Utilizing trial or drop-in classes

Try classes at a few different studios before deciding on your final decision and signing a contract for kids ages 3 to 18. It lets your dancer try a class and see if they like the class, teacher, and even if they like ballet. Not all schools offer trial or drop-in classes, but it never hurts to ask about them.

Tip 3: Usually, you can take a trial class before signing a contract.

Children and teens that have narrowed down their studio search should take at least one class at the studio you or your child has chosen. A trial class is an option at studios, and it doesn't hurt to ask if your child can come to class one day as a trial to see if they like the classes at that studio. These trial courses are usually free, or you will be asked to pay around $20.00 for the class. Taking a trial class lets your child try a studio before signing up. Ballet studios make students and parents sign a contract stating how much they will be expected to pay per month and a yearly total. These contracts also include the name of the parent or family member who will usually bring kids to and from class, emergency contact numbers, and the child's medical conditions. Not all studios have contracts, but it is a common thing you will encounter at some point.

There is a lot of flexibility for adults regarding trial classes. All adult classes are considered "Drop-In Classes," which means you pay per class. Your first class or first few lessons can be taken on a trial basis. Adult classes understand that sometimes life gets in the way, and you may have to miss a class. For example, suppose you find ballet isn't what you thought it would be or isn't enjoyable. In that case, you can find another place to dance or stop without breaking any contracts. The standard cost per class for adults is around $20.00 per class, and many studios offer a class pack you can purchase instead. These class packs or class cards provide X number of classes per month cards that you have paid for in advance. One of these packs or cards usually starts at $100, but it allows you to not worry about having cash or writing checks before each class. It is becoming more common for studios to offer packs or cards when you register for a course online.

For both children and adults, choose the studio that feels right. All studios teach in different ways, have teachers that are strict or a bit more relaxed, and have other classes and times to attend. If a studio doesn't feel like a good fit, you can leave. If you choose to go for a contract-required studio, you may have to pay off the month or semester. Ballet class should be fun, a place to grow as a person, and a place to challenge yourself and your body. Trust your gut and go with the studio that feels right for your child or yourself.

What should I look for in a studio when it comes to classes?

All studios are not created equally; the same can be said about classes. These recommendations are just recommendations. I have been a ballet teacher for several years and went to a strict studio known for producing professional dancers. I can provide some suggestions of what to look for regarding class structure and difficulty level. The most important thing for any ballet studio is for its students to be taught proper ballet techniques and terminology. Without technique, there is no ballet. The style, methods, and positions in ballet have been refined over hundreds of years and are still taught the same way today. If you have a background in ballet and learn the technique, you can dance any other dance style; ballet is the foundation of dance. Learning the terminology allows a dancer to understand what an instructor is asking them to do and how to speak about choreography.

Tip 4: Things to look for in classes for students ages 3 to 8 years old.

When your child is between the ages of 3 and 8 years old, there are a few things to consider when choosing the best dance studio for them to attend. Ballet has a strict set of rules and expectations. The class must be less based on play and more on learning for dancers in this age range. The classes will still be fun, but students aren't running around playing. Technique is always needed. I cannot stress this enough, but when a dancer is young and starting their ballet adventure, learning the technique will make them safer, smarter, and stronger.

Some studios are often called "boutique studios," which typically only teach students from 18 months to 7 years old. These boutique studios are different from traditional dance studios. These studios are more about playing and do not place as much emphasis on solid technique. There is nothing wrong with boutique studios, but they tend to be less structured and not as technique-based. I was an instructor in one of these boutique studios in San Francisco a few years back. There were so many activities I had to do with the kids besides dancing (read stories, play, color, etc.). I never had enough time to teach my students the technique they needed to know during class. I highly recommend enrolling your child in a ballet school instead if they really want to learn ballet.

Tip 5: Things to look for in classes for students ages 8 to 13 years old.

When your child is between 8 to 13 years old, the dancing becomes more advanced. Again, the best studio to dance at should focus on technique and have a pointe program. If possible, find out the age of students for dancing en pointe (en pointe = on pointe). The technique gets more advanced for students to prepare for pointe work in this age range. If your child is starting and are these ages, it is important to let the studio owner know your child is a beginner. They may place your child in a much younger class to learn basics or suggest private lessons. Starting ballet at this age does not mean your child can't become a professional dancer. But you need to be realistic with your child, inform them that it is possible if they work hard and are very serious about being a professional when they are 18 or 19.

Most studios will have children start "pre-pointe" at about 10 or 11 years old. These classes are designed to strengthen your child's feet and ankles. Typical exercises in these classes are all based on developing the muscles of the feet and ankles—exercises such as raising up and down on both legs, a single leg, and balancing longer. While the age of dancers en pointe varies, it is considered medically safe to start pointe at 12 years old. Taking pre-pointe classes for a year or longer is strategically done to build the student's strength before putting on a pair of pointe shoes. If you see younger children, ten years old or younger, in pointe shoes, the students may not be strong enough for pointe work. Opinions on the age at which a student should begin pointe work vary by studio, country, or ballet program. When a child is in this age range, they are eligible to compete in the Youth American Grand Prix, as well and do so en pointe.

Tip 6: Things to look for in classes for students ages 13 to 18 years old.

Between the ages of 13 to 18, the studio you choose depends on two factors. The first is the child's previous dance history. The second is if they want to pursue a professional dance career. Beginners or "late start" dancers should consider enrolling in private one-on-one coaching. This means your dancer will not be placed in a class with young beginners. Instead, they will be in a lesson alone with a teacher. Private lessons guarantee the proper attention to the dancer. Private lessons allow a teacher and the dancer set specific goals for each class. If private lessons are not in your budget, inquire if your dancer can join any adult beginner classes at the studio. It is possible for a beginner or "late start" student to become a professional dancer. American Ballet Theater's principal dancer (the highest-ranked in the company), Misty Copeland, began her ballet journey at 13 years old. She then became the first black woman to be a principal dancer in the history of the American Ballet Theater.

Make sure your teen understands the amount of work they need to do in order to become a professional dancer. Hard work and dedication are two significant factors for training to be a professional. Attending Summer Intensives at professional companies and competing in national and international ballet competitions can be very beneficial. Summer Intensives (SI) are audition-based ballet "sleep-away camps." Instead of swimming in a lake and doing arts and craft projects, attendees spend somewhere between 8 - 10 hours dancing. These programs vary in cost and length of the program.

Most professional dance companies have programs and being able to say something like, "I went to Joffrey in '08 and '10, ABT in '09, '11, and '12. I auditioned for and was accepted into Kirov in Russia, Royal Ballet, and Alvin Ailey's junior program and their senior program" is a big deal and looks impressive on a dance resume. Since ballet companies all over the world have SI's and welcome students from anywhere, you will make friends with dancers from anywhere and everywhere. SI's allow dancers to work with some of the best dance teachers in the ballet world. If the instructors at the

SI see potential or want to keep working with you, they may offer a scholarship for next summer or a spot in their year-round pre-professional program.

If your dancer just wants to dance for fun and not pursue a career in ballet, you can attend the same programs. Many local dance studios offer "dance camps" structured like a summer intensive, but you participate for the day and return home in the evenings. For example, when I went to the second studio I danced at as a teen, I attended their dance camp to test out the classes, meet the teachers, and see what other dance styles were taught. It helped me decide to stay at that studio and allowed me to meet other dancers at the school.

Many dancers who do not want to be professional ballet dancers go to SIs as well. I attended a week-long ballet-only intensive program at the Interlochen Center for the Arts in Michigan. I spent almost 7-8 hours dancing with fantastic instructors and felt that my dancing started to change for the better. As much as I wanted to spend my entire summer at Interlochen, it was not something my family could afford for another 6-8 weeks. So it was a surprise when I got a letter from the school a few weeks after the camp ended. I was offered a spot in their Arts Academy to finish my last three years of high school. It felt amazing to have been there a week and know that I did well enough to get a spot in a prestigious fine arts school. I didn't accept the offer because I wanted to stay in the marching band, and my parents had always insisted that I had to go to college and earn a degree first before trying to be a professional dancer.

If your teen wants to train for fun and has no intention of pursuing a career as a professional, that is okay. That is a common occurrence and won't be any issues when selecting a studio. Older teen dancers also can attend adult or open ballet classes. Many colleges with a dance program will offer ballet classes for non-dance majors. These classes are sometimes full of musical theater majors and super fun. These classes also permit students to wear pointe shoes if they choose to. Professors will allow more advanced dancers to add more challenging things to the exercises like jumps with leg beats or more turns than required, etc. I took "Advanced Ballet for Non-Majors" classes at Florida State University each semester I was in college.

If you are considering a professional career, there are very specific things that a studio needs to offer. Along with technique having former professionals as instructors and variation classes are perfect. Former professionals will have first-hand experience and can be a source for advice when considering a career as a professional. Variation class is when the dancers are taught a solo from classical ballets in a group. Some variations can be used as solos for competitions or auditions for summer intensive programs. Some of the ballets the variations can come from include: Sleep Beauty, Coppelia, Don Quixote, La Bayadère, Swan Lake, and many more.

It is worth considering joining a Pre-Professional, Trainee, or Conservatory program if a teen wants to be a professional. These programs involve attending a boarding school or going to your studio starting at 8 am. The dancers will have a designated time for schoolwork through virtual school. After their school time is over, they will start dance classes for the rest of the afternoon and evening. It is typical for 4-5 hours a day to be devoted to school and then taking dance classes from noon or 1 pm until 9:30 every day. The evenings after classes are over are when the students are to do homework or study for their classes.

If the studio participates in dance competitions, the type of competition is important. Competitions with other styles besides ballet and contemporary are fun. However, those competitions will not push a ballet career further along. Ballet-based competitions are what a student need. In a ballet-based competition, dancers must perform a classical solo. Some ask competitors to take a class as well where they will be evaluated and scored at the end of the competition. This is a shortlist of the most prestigious competitions to attend:

- Prix de Lausanne
- International Ballet Competition (IBC)
- Varna IBC
- Universal Ballet Competition (UBC)
- World Ballet Competition (WBC)
- Helsinki International Ballet Competition
- Youth American Grand Prix (YAGP)

You can become a successful professional ballet dancer without participating in competitions. You don't have to want to dance professionally to compete in these competitions. These competitions are networking and talent scouting opportunities. These competitions are where professional company directors or other staff attend to see if any dancer is someone they want to come dance for them professionally. Scholarships for intensives or contracts to join a company or several companies are common "prizes" a dancer can win at competitions, along with a first, second, or third medal and plaque.

Can I ask people I know which studios they like?

You can always ask people if they recommend a studio if you know their children are dancers. Keep in mind some of the elements in classes you should look for or inquire upon from the above tips.

Tip 7: Sometimes, asking for recommendations for studios can produce excellent results.

Suppose you are still trying to find the proper ballet studio for you or your child to attend. Posting on Facebook and Community Facebook pages asking for studio recommendations is a good idea. Asking for recommendations can help narrow down your search. It can also provide more information about dancers' experiences at a particular studio. Asking for recommendations is helpful for children but do a bit of additional research. Using social media to ask for a studio for adults can produce a list of studios that other adult dancers are attending. It never hurts to ask for recommendations and save yourself a long and tedious google deep dive.

Chapter 1 Review

- Finding a ballet class for young students is a breeze, but adults may have a difficult time.
- Search on Google for studios near you and read the reviews or ask on Facebook for recommendations of studios
- Take advantage of trial and drop-in classes to try out a studio before committing to one.
- Adult ballet classes are always drop-in classes because sometimes work or life can get in the way of attending a class. The standard drop-in rate is around $20.00 per class.
- From the age of 3 to 103, learning the proper technique is essential to dancing ballet safely. A technique-based studio is the best route to take when choosing a studio to attend.
- If your child is considering a career as a professional ballet dancer, competing in national and international ballet competitions can lead to scholarships and contracts from ballet companies across the globe.

Chapter 2: Time to Look the Part

Like all other sports, ballet requires the right equipment and wardrobe. The "uniform" for girls, boys, and adults has been designed with mobility in mind and worn for centuries. There is a widely accepted standard of dress for ballet classes across the globe which we will go through.

Should I wear a tutu and crown to my first class?

No, but it is important to discuss what to wear to dance class. You wouldn't go to football practice without pads and a helmet. Ballet is the same. You wouldn't dance without shoes and tights. It's best to look at the part.

Tip 8: Find out the dress code at your studio and follow it.

Most studios, including those requiring signing a contract, will have a set dress code. Specific requirements for how their students should be dressed when attending classes will be included. In contracts and on the website for the studio, there will usually be a list of what to wear for all ages. If your studio doesn't have a detailed dress code, there is a general "uniform" for children and adults.

Tip 9: What to wear if you are a girl between 3 to 13 years old.

Black leotards, pink tights, and ballet shoes are standards for what you would wear to class at this age. Many styles and cuts of leotards can make a plain black leotard match your personality. Some dance studios may use colored leotards. Each class will have a specific color assigned to its level. This gives students more options for "fun leotards" they are permitted to wear. Other accessories like skirts are up to the teacher to decide. Although, as a former dance teacher,

I know how cute the little pink, purple or blue leotards with attached skirts are at a dancewear store, I do not recommend it for dancers under the age of 10. The skirt tends to be a distraction for younger students; they like to play with the skirt instead of using their "ballet arms."

No matter what age, underwear is not worn under tights when dressing for class! From a dance teacher's perspective, it makes the legs and hips look lumpy. They also make it harder to be sure they are using the correct muscles from an early age. Another reason underwear is not worn under your tights is that they tend to hang down past the leg of the leotard. In addition, having your underwear showing is not polite, and it doesn't look "professional." Finally, little kids tend to find underwear under their tights irritating. They constantly adjust their underwear and tend to participate far less.

Ballet is an old art form with some core rules. Over time, these rules have not changed, including rules about wearing a leotard, tights, nothing under your tights but your body, and hair should be up in a bun.

Tip 10: Write your name or put your initials in your ballet shoes.

One of the most common items a dancer loses is their ballet shoes. Writing the student's first/last name or initials inside the shoe is one way to keep track of them. Especially when there is a group of eleven 5-year-olds who all have the same pair of shoes. It is important to note that ballet shoes of all kinds do not have a right or left side. However, the shoes will start to take shape based on the foot it is worn on. Dancers prefer to wear the shoes they have designated as the right and left. (A right and left shoe assignment is important for pointe shoes.) The heat from dancing makes your feet sweat, making the leather shoes mold to the shape of the foot.

HowExpert Advice: Younger dancers who are still learning their lefts and rights can work on that skill with their ballet shoes! Write a small R or L in the shoes under their name or initials so they can practice even at their ballet classes.

Tip 11: Cut the elastic "antennas" and avoid glitter-encrusted shoes.

Ballet shoes have an elastic (or cloth) drawstring at the top of the shoe used to tighten or loosen their shoes. These elastics are very long and are expected to be cut, tied, and tucked into the shoe. When cut too short, the drawstrings get lost in the binding of the shoes, like a drawstring on a sweatshirt in the dryer. The best method of dealing with elastics for children who don't know how to tie their shoes is to cut the "antennas." Then, tie them in a bow that can be tucked into the top of the shoe comfortably. Next, cut only a few inches off the ends of the bow and tie knots at the ends of each elastic. The best way to secure the shoes would be with a double knot to keep the elastics from popping out of the shoe. This will ensure the elastic won't move and are a more reasonable size to tie for little dancers.

I have often worked with "baby ballerinas," and two things slow classes down. The first is when one child needs to use the restroom; all the dancers suddenly need to go as well, which requires helping them get out of their leotards and a boost to get on the commode. The second thing is tying everyone's shoes when they become untied. And baby ballerinas love to untie their elastics and want the teacher to re-tie them. With the length the elastics come in, they will inevitably pop out of their tucked position. Tripping, slipping, or having someone else step on your dancer's loose antennas is common. Cutting and tying the elastics is the best way to prevent an accident or an injury.

HowExpert advice: Your child may not like it, but the bow needs to be tucked under the front of the shoe and on top of the dancer's foot. Dancers or parents of young dancers with sensory disorders or sensitivities, let your teacher know. We will allow the bows to be outside of the shoe or permit alternative uniforms for students who need them.

In recent years, I have seen little ones wearing shoes encrusted with pink or gold glitter. While these shoes are cute and your dancer may want them, it is best to avoid them. They shed glitter everywhere and are stiffer than regular leather shoes. The adhesive used on these shoes makes them inflexible and limits the ability of a dancer to point her feet. Many other costume parts will be covered in glitter; the shoes are best left in their plain pink color.

Tip 12: Older dancers may be permitted to wear colored leotards or accessories.

In many studios, each class will have a specific color assigned to their level. Royal blue and a specific brand and style of leotards were something you earned when you joined the advanced dancers at my first studio. Color assignments give students more options for "fun leotards" that they are permitted to wear. Studios may also allow wearing a colored leotard on a particular class day or during rehearsals. If you are unsure if wearing colored leotards is permitted at your studio, just ask a teacher. It never hurts to ask or receive clarification on the approved dress code. Baby Ballerinas (They are big girls and will let you know it) are going to be picky. Having them with you to try things on is wise. I'm selective with my leotards and the fabric they are made of. Dancers can be drama queens and kings at times.

Tip 13: Accessories - Warm-up gear or approved for class accessories.

Older dancers, usually teens, may be allowed to wear dance "accessories." These accessories can be divided into warm-ups or class permitted accessories. The amount of warm-up clothes that dancers wear is up to them. Professional dancers take classes in so many layers that they look like they are wearing snowsuits. The purpose of warm-up clothing is to warm up the muscles and joints of the body at a quicker rate. These clothes can warm the joints and muscles a bit more than the first few exercises of a ballet class will do alone. At many studios, your warm-ups are typically permitted for the first two or three exercises at the barre. After that, they are expected to be removed. Typical warm-up gear includes a variety of things. Some popular items are legwarmers, garbage bag pants, vests, booties, fuzzy socks worn over pointe shoes, and scarves.

Class permitted accessories differ for each studio and are usually stated in the studio's dress code rules. The class-allowed accessories are generally far less bulky than warm-up gear. Class-approved items include wrap skirts, hip alignment belts, and practice tutus. Not all these things are permitted. Each studio decides what accessories its students are allowed to wear to classes. If a dance teacher asks you or your child to remove accessories, it should be done immediately.

Tip 14: Standard attire for boys and young men.

Almost all dance studios have the same basic "uniform" for their male dancers. The uniform consists of black tights, a black or white T-shirt, and black or white canvas ballet shoes. For younger boys, some studios allow them to wear athletic shorts for classes. For young men who have been through puberty, wearing a dance belt is required. A dance belt is an underwear-like garment worn to keep genitals out of the way of the legs. If your child needs a dance belt, give them a few days at home to wear it and get used to it.

Many dance websites provide sizing information and how to wear the belt properly. For example, wearing spandex shorts is permitted for teens, but it isn't standard. See the uniform requirements in your contract or on the studio's website when in doubt.

Tip 15: What to wear for adult women.

For female adult dancers, the attire for a class is much more flexible than for younger dancers. Studios ask you to wear leggings, yoga pants, a form-fitting shirt, or a tank top if you don't want to wear a leotard. Wear either flat ballet shoes or thick socks on your feet. This suggested wardrobe allows the body to move freely, but the teacher can still see your body. Not every adult feels comfortable wearing a leotard or tights. Adult classes know that and want you to feel comfortable. Adult dancers can also wear leotards and tights if they want to. The standard leotard and tights combination is flexible as well. Any color leotard is acceptable, and you can wear a variety of tights in color or style. Any solid color of tights is permitted. Adult dancers can also wear any dance accessories, such as wrap skirts or warm-up gear. Hair is not required to be in a bun, just pulled back away from the face. For adult women, the goal is to feel comfortable moving and attending class.

Tip 16: What to wear for adult men.

Similar to the clothing options for women, the recommended attire for men is all about comfort and movability: sweat pants, athletic shorts, a T-shirt or tank top, socks, or ballet shoes. Adult men can also wear tights, spandex shorts, and plain white or black shirts. One recommended thing for adult male dancers of any level is wearing a dance belt. I've heard adult male dancers say, "The only thing worse than dancing in a dance belt would be dancing without one." They do take some getting used to for all ages.

Tip 17: A dance bag is always a must-have!

A dance bag is an essential item for dancers of all ages. Unfortunately, ballet shoes tend to get lost. Regardless of how old you are, they tend to go missing for a bit or forever. If your shoes live in your dance bag, the chance of losing one is significantly decreased. Beyond holding your shoes, a dance bag has everything a dancer thinks they will need for class and protects wallets and keys, so they are kept safe while you dance. Some studios have a specific room with cubbyholes for dancers to put their bags in. Others let you bring your bag into the studio. If you attend class at a studio that permits bringing your bag into the room, make sure your bags are against a wall and are out of the way. What your bag looks like or contains is up to the dancer. There are a few recommendations I want to make for young, teen, and adult ballet dancers to add to their dance bag.

What should I put in my dance bag?

Tip 18: Dance bag recommendation for young dancers.

As a former ballet teacher, what your young dancer has in their bag should be things to prepare them for class. It is a good idea for very young dancers to have a bag with a clean set of "street clothing" (non-dance clothes) and one or two pairs of underwear. Many children want to change from their leotards and tights once the class is over. Having an extra set of clothes on hand can come in handy. When your dancer is between 2 to 4 years old, sometimes, they will have an accident.

Some dancers don't want to stop or leave class to go to the bathroom. Others are shy and won't mention that they need to use the bathroom, and an accident can happen. Having a spare set of dry clothes (dance or street clothing) to change your little one into and send them back to class as if nothing happened is something I strongly recommend. If your dance teacher is angry or punishes your dancer for having an accident in class, find a new studio. Any dance teacher who works with "baby ballerinas" expects at least one accident. It happens, and cleaning up and not making a scene is standard protocol. Make sure the student is in dry clothing of some sort and is calm and returns to class, or is the "dance teacher helper" in the room if they don't want to participate after their accident.

I love teaching "baby ballet" classes and had a little one come up to me asking to go to the bathroom and urinate on my feet because they waited too long to ask to go to the bathroom or were "having too much fun." It has happened to me more times than I care to think about. You can include a plastic bag with another leotard and tights in case of an accident.

When students are allowed to get water or if they can keep it in the room with them depends on each studio. Still, it is always a good idea to include a bottle of water or a travel cup that, if knocked over, won't make a big puddle on the floor. Your dancer will likely want some water after class, and having a water bottle in their bag lets them do just that. This also prepares them for knowing what to take to class when they are older.

Having extra bun and hair supplies is a must-have in any dance bag. Sometimes students are brought to class by a parent who usually doesn't take them. Most of the time, the other parent (usually fathers or older brothers) doesn't know how to make a proper bun. Having supplies and a brush in the dance bag lets other parents or older dancers help fix your child's hair. I like to use a small tin (I have always used an empty Altoid mints box) to put extra hair ties, bobby pins, and clips inside. This saves you from trying to find them at the bottom of the dance bag. For older children, hair supplies are a must. Dance bags have a way of being too small to fit everything and, at the same time, an endless black hole.

HowExpert Advice: In a creative movement, pre-ballet, or beginning ballet classes, parents should expect minor accidents. Not just waiting too long to mention they need the bathroom, but almost everything else. Toddlers toddle around, fall over for fun, fall over on accident, trip, step on someone else's toes or fingers, you name it. It's a group of toddlers excited to dance, and well, toddlers are not known for their balancing skills. So, hearing your child say something like, "Alexis stepped on Jessica's hand on accident and cried, so I gave her a hug," is normal. Many dance teachers are CPR certified and know how to deal with accidents big and small. Your tiny dancer is in safe hands.

Tip 19: Dance bag recommendations for tween and teen dancers.

When dancers are 7 through 18 years old, they should know what to keep in their bags. Beyond basics like shoes, water, and feminine products, there are a few things a dancer will be glad to have in their bag.

It is always wise to have extra bun supplies, especially if the dancer comes straight from school to the studio and needs to put their hair up. For teens who are en pointe, a small sewing kit is necessary. The dancer has to sew their elastics and ribbons onto the pointe shoes. There should be dental floss or waxed thread made for pointe shoes in a dancer's sewing kit, two or three thicker needles, a thimble, a lighter, and if they have any, spare ribbons. Dance supply websites and stores will have a small tube containing the standard waxed thread for pointe shoes and a few needles. You can grab one of these little kits or use white dental floss. Ribbons and elastics can unravel and become satin threads at an astonishingly fast once they have been cut. To solve this, all your dancers will use a lighter. Hold a lighter underneath the cut parts of the ribbon or elastic to melt the satin or rubber to seal the edge. While you might not want your teen to have a lighter, one for dance is necessary.

Adding a TheraBand for warming up the feet before class is common in older dancers' bags. Some dancers like to wear ankle weights to class for strength building. A set of two- or three-pound weights can go in a dance bag as well. While a teacher might recommend ankle weights for students who have weak ankle and foot strength, it is not a punishment. Extending your leg off the floor while wearing weights forces a dancer to use their abdominals to hold the leg there instead of gripping in the hips and thighs. I had to wear them because I have naturally hyperextended knees. My legs bow backward when I straighten my legs. As a result, my knees overextend, which changes how my body holds positions and can cause injuries. Weights are used to keep the dancer aware of their ankles rolling and when the legs are together, not fully extending their leg when standing. The weights are bulky enough to force the dancer to relax the knee when standing.

Extra or a pair of leg warmers or ankle and foot braces or wraps are often found in dance bags. Icy-Hot, Bengay, or BioFreeze is a great product to keep in teen's dance bags. Sore muscles from the many classes and long rehearsals are unfortunate parts of ballet. Having a product for their aching muscles will be appreciated before their next class or the next rehearsal.

Keeping a tiny travel-sized deodorant in their dance bag is good for any dancer. I haven't met a dancer who does not have deodorant in their bags to use at the studio. The studios can be very warm before class even starts. It's seen as respectful to everyone to wear deodorant if needed. If your dancer doesn't want to use deodorant, that is okay, but I recommend they try it before class. A small bag or tin or pocket in the dance bag filled with Band-Aids is also a good idea. Sometimes your dancer will need them for blisters when starting pointe classes. For dancers who have been through puberty, a bag with feminine products is necessary. This bag is great for your dancer and if anyone in their class needs a product as well. Finally, all dance shoes should be in the bag or on your dancer's feet. Being prepared with the clothes and shoes you need is a lesson ballet teaches children. Learning responsibility for your things and being prepared at a young age is a good life skill.

Tip 20: Dance bag recommendations for adult dancers.

As an adult dancer, you will always have your shoes or an extra pair of socks, at least one hair tie, and water. Things from your purse like a wallet and keys as well can be held in a dance bag. Icy-Hot, Bengay, or BioFreeze are great things to keep in your dance bag. You will likely be sore the next few days after your first class. Trust me, that Icy-Hot is your godsend. Applying some product to your body before your class if you are still sore from the previous class you took can help relieve the pain. For dancers who get sweaty when they dance, throw a washcloth or rag into your bag. If you need to wipe your face, it will be right there, and you can do it quickly.

Tip 21: What you put in your dance bag is up to you, and there is no right or wrong way to prepare your bag for class.

Once you have taken a few ballet classes, you will be able to decide what you want or don't want in your dance bag. As long as you have your dance shoes and appropriate dancewear, anything else you toss into your dance bag is up to you.

The Proper Ballet Bun

Picture a ballerina in your mind and look at how her hair is styled. It is a bun! Buns are the preferred hairstyle for classes and performances. Some professionals put their hair into a French twist, but buns are the most common style. The bun serves several different purposes for dancers. When turning, loose hair can get tangled up if left down or will whip your face or your partner's face if it is long enough. During classes, a bun allows dancers and teachers to see their shoulders, upper back, and face. In addition, a bun keeps younger and even older dancers from constantly playing with their hair during class. Here are some tips for making your ballet bun.

Before we start, I would like to take a moment to discus
should be done for girls with very short hair or braids a
or protective hairstyles. For girls with short hair like a
bob and girls with natural hair, you might not be able
hair into a bun. Wearing a headband to hold your hair back ...
work just as well as a bun. You are okay for girls with braids or
other protective styles as long as your hair is pulled back and won't
come undone. If a studio tells you that your child can't wear
protective styles, braids, extensions, or anything else, you turn
around and walk out the door.

Tip 22: Bun Supplies.

You will need a few supplies to make your bun. Here is what you
need:

- Hairbrush
- Two elastic hair ties
- Bobby pins (there are never enough bobby pins)
- Bun net
- Hair clips that match the color of your hair
- Spray bottle of water
- Hairspray

Tip 23: Pull the hair into a high ponytail in the middle of the head or higher up on the head.

A bun starts with a high ponytail, and it is the anchor for bobby pins
as well.

Tip 24: For dancers with thin or fine hair.

Hold your head upside down for dancers with thin and fine hair and
dampen the hair closest to the scalp. While making the ponytail,
hold your hair in one hand. With the other hand, spray the damp
areas of your head with a little bit of hairspray. Then brush the hair
into the ponytail. With wet hair, the hairspray will be softer and
help you shape a ponytail. I have thin and fine hair. Making a bun
for a while was a pain because my hair would fall out of my grasp,
or the hair tie wouldn't stay in place. I tried the method I described

ve and found that it gave me more control of my hair. Starting a
n like this has made the process of bun-making easier. If you
have thin or fine hair, consider using this method. You don't have to
do it like this, but this is how I've made my buns for the last 17
years.

Tip 25: Time to twist and wrap.

Take the hair in the ponytail and twist the hair tightly—coil the
twisted hair around the base of the ponytail. How long or thick your
hair is will determine the number of times your hair will wrap about
itself.

Tip 26: Have bobby pins at the ready.

Depending on how long your hair it's helpful to pin your hair as you
wrap it. Take the bobby pin and put one tip of the pin into the bun
halfway down or closer to the head. The other tip of the pin will
slide into the hair underneath the hair tie and lock the hair in place.

Once you have pined and wrapped, you will need to add more pins.
Add more bobby pins if the bun feels loose anywhere or is not
solidly pressed into the scalp. Keep adding pins until it feels like you
could replicate the headbanging scene from Wayne's World. The
bun will not move an inch if it is securely fastened.

Tip 27: The bun net. (If you don't need one, skip to Tip 28)

For kids at dance schools that do require a bun net, this is the next
step in the bun process for you. You can usually find bun nets at
grocery stores in the haircare area or order them on amazon. First,
find a net that matches your hair color as best as possible, and then
stretch the net open with both hands. Then move both hands back
and put one part of the net around your bun. Next, twist the net
once and loop it over the bun again. Then take the excess net and
tuck it under the outermost coil of your bun. You can cut the net in
half and use one half at a time for little kids. The nets prevent fly-
away- hairs, but they are fragile. Be careful removing your bun net
and your bobby pins when you take out your bun after class. The

net gets snagged, and holes are ripped into the net. If you or your child needs to use bun nets, buy a few at a time. There are thicker bun nets, but they are suitable for performances or if you or your child has very thick hair—these last longer.

Tip 28: Completing the bun.

If you use a bun net or not, this is always the last step. If you want to prevent fly-away-hairs, lightly mist your hair around your face with some hairspray. Next, use hair clips to sweep up hair at the nape of your neck and clip it under your bun. If your bun still feels loose, try putting a plain elastic over the bun to tighten the entire bun. Little girls can wear colorful scrunchies around the bun at many ballet schools. Girls gradually stop putting the colorful scrunchies over their buns around 11. When shopping for a cute scrunchie for your bun, it should not be a distraction to your child or other dancers in the room.

You are now ready for class with your proper attire, fully stocked dance bag, and the perfect ballet bun!

Chapter 2 Review

- What to wear for class - Children
- What to wear for class - Teens
- What to wear for class - Adults
- Items to keep in your dance bag to be ready for class.
- How to make the perfect ballet bun.
- Advice for dancers with short hair or braids and protective styles.
- Being responsible for your personal belongings and prepared for class is a skill you will learn by taking ballet classes.

Chapter 3: Ballet Etiquette

Ballet has been around for centuries. Because of that, specific rules or ways to act have become universal in every dance studio. Learning the proper etiquette for a ballet class can also be applied in regular life outside of a dance studio. Ballet teaches respect for others and those in charge and how body language says more than words can. Ask for help when you need it and how important it can be to be ready and early for things. While this chapter has many do's and don'ts, it is the one chapter that you do not want to skip, no matter how old you are.

Respect is fundamental in the dance world, not only in ballet classes. Some studios are incredibly strict about ballet etiquette. Others encourage it but aren't strict about minor things like not having a bun net in your hair during class. I went to a strict ballet studio in Florida when I was growing up. Respecting the rules, your instructors, and yourself was a very serious thing at that studio. For example,

We were not allowed to have holes in our tights. Ever. If the studio owner saw someone with a hole in their tights walking by her desk, she would not let you take the class. You were breaking the dress code, and that was against the rules. If you had an extra pair of tights without holes in your dance bag, you were sent to change into those tights as fast as humanly possible.

If you didn't have an extra pair in your dance bag, you were kicked out for the entire class. When a parent would come to pick up the students who couldn't drive, they would see you sitting there. Not in class where you are supposed to be and instead are sitting on a bench in the lobby. You then would have to explain why you weren't in class to your parent or whoever came to pick you up. If you were in a class taught by the studio owner and she saw even the smallest hole in your tights, she would stick her finger into the hole. Then pull the hole to make it bigger and kick you out for the rest of the class. She would do this even if she popped her head in the door, looked in on a class she wasn't even teaching and saw a hole.

Looking back on this now, I realize it sounds like something crazy to do to a child. But it was just how things were at that studio. This studio was known for being the best in the area. All teachers were current or former professional dancers. The studio was also known for making professional dancers. Having holes in our tights or not being prepared for every class was seen as rude. The hole was disrespectful to your teacher, the entire class, and yourself.

Proper etiquette doesn't start when you are a professional ballet dancer. It begins when your foot passes through the doorway and into the studio. If that studio was still open and I had a child who wanted to start dance lessons, I would send them to that studio. I still use and value the lessons and etiquette I learned and practiced from 3 to 18. I wouldn't be the woman I am today if I hadn't gone to that studio.

General Etiquette for Ballet Classes

Tip 29: Always be on time.

While ballet class is set up to warm up your body with each exercise, it's always good to stretch a bit before the class starts. Arriving at the studio 15-30 minutes before your class is ideal for warming up before class. If you can't go into the studio room because another class is inside, you can warm up in any spare space you can find. Being early also means you have time to get dressed and put your shoes on before you are allowed to enter the room.

At some ballet schools, the teacher will close the door to the studio room at the official start of class on the dot. This means that class has started, and anyone who comes late won't be able to take the class. If you arrive late, quietly and quickly jump into position at the closest spot at the barre. Wait at the door until the exercise has been done on both sides. Then quietly get to the barre.

Sometimes people are late. You name it, be it getting stuck in traffic, oversleeping, or losing the keys to the car. It is not the end of the world if you are 10 or 15 minutes late to class. There are things you can't control, and that is understandable. However, if you are always late, that is a problem that needs to be solved.

As one of my former dance teachers liked to say:

"If you arrive on time, you are already 15 minutes late" - Joan Miller.

Tip 30: No talking (unless you have to).

A ballet performance is a silent art where your body tells a story instead of your voice. Class is the same way. However, there are times when talking in class has to be done unless there is an issue or injury.

Lots of talking can make hearing what your teacher said difficult. I hate to break it to you, but whispering is louder than you think, especially in a dance class. There is a time for fun and chatting with your friends, and that is before or after class. It is disrespectful to your teacher and the other dancers. You are allowed to laugh when it is appropriate (never at someone when they make a mistake). Sometimes your teacher will do something funny on purpose. Maybe demonstrate how the class was dancing by over-exaggerating or explaining. That is a time when laughing and playing are okay.

Tip 31: Be mindful of your body language.

When in class, your dance teacher watches and looks at every student. How a dancer holds their body when they aren't dancing is as important as it is when they are dancing.

As mentioned earlier, ballet is about respecting and respecting your instructors. Dancers who slump and lean against the barres give the impression that they are bored. They don't care to be there, are tired, and won't try as hard as they should. The other ballet class body language to avoid is crossing your arms in front of your chest.

When you see someone at work or speak to someone with arms crossed, it is natural to assume that the person is mad. The same is true in ballet class. It's better to stand with your hands on your hips or with a hand on the barre. Not all teachers are strict about some of these body language behaviors. That is fine when you take their classes, but other teachers won't be the same. If you go to a masterclass or another studio for another class, it is always better to keep this tip in mind.

It is always better to be polite and aware of your body and how you carry yourself.

Tip 32: Yawning.

A general rule in ballet class is not to let your teacher see you yawn. Yawning is a natural human activity, and you can't stop when your body yawns. Dance teachers aren't asking you not to yawn. They want you to do it politely, quietly and draw as little attention to yourself. You or your child won't get in trouble if a yawn happens. It's just polite to do it discretely.

Tip 33: Watching the clock/Asking about the time.

This is a pet peeve of most dance instructors. If there is a clock in the studio, all dancers focus on it. It looks like you cannot wait to leave, and there is no subtle way of watching the clock while you dance. Many dance studios have a clock in the lobby and none in the studios. It is typical for a ballet class to run a few minutes past the scheduled end of class.

Teachers aren't constantly watching the clock and often lose track of time. If you are still in class and dancing after class is supposed to end, it will usually be only a few minutes. If it is 15 or 20 minutes after class is scheduled to finish, you can mention that the class is over. But if you are over a minute or two, don't run out the studio door.

If you know you have to leave class early, it is best to inform your teacher before class starts. Letting them know in advance is your responsibility as a dancer. They might not be looking at the time and don't realize it is time for you to go. Walking out of class before it is over is looked down upon. If you have to finish class early, you should walk out quickly and quietly. If you are an adult dancer and have to leave early, let your teacher know right away. Dance teachers understand that life happens, and sometimes you have to leave early. They understand you may have to run out to pick up your child from soccer practice when you are an adult dancer.

Tip 34: NO GUM!

Chewing gum in class is rude, but it is also gross. Nobody wants to watch you chew gum the entire class. Dancing while chewing gum is also very dangerous. Every dance teacher will tell the students the same "story":

"Once, during a rehearsal, a man and woman were rehearsing their pas de deux. When he went to lift her over his head, he choked on the gum. He was turning blue, and they tried to get the gum out of his throat by cutting into his neck to pull it out so he could breathe. Unfortunately, it was stuck, and it was so far down in his throat that nobody could pull the gum out. He didn't make it; he bled to death on the studio floor. And that is why we do not chew gum in class."

This story is made up, but teachers use it to scare the kids into not chewing gum during class; telling this tale of the dancer who chewed gum and died works well. Teachers will tell stories like that, and the kids in class will never try to dance with gum in their mouths again. It works every time. Adult dancers won't hear the same story but will be asked to spit their gum out.

Etiquette for Barre

Every ballet class starts with dancing at the barre. Each combination you do at the barre warms up your body muscle by muscle. A teacher of mine once said, *"If you are not drenched in sweat by the second or third combination, you are not working hard enough."* Barre is essential, and there are a few rules all dancers will learn as they keep taking classes. I will share them with you now.

Tip 35: Stand with enough space between you and the dancers in front and behind you.

The ideal distance between yourself and the others at the barre is large enough, so you will not kick the other dancers. Older dancers are taught that they need to turn their feet and body into or away from the barre if the barre is crowded. This is done to prevent kicking others. It involves angling your body and feet slightly away from the barre when extending to the front. Then turn your body and feet towards the barre to extend the leg to the back. Being at an angle means your leg moves away from the dancers in front of and behind you.

There will be accidents where you kick someone or get hit with a foot in a tap or pointe shoe. It is inevitable, but making sure you have enough space decreases the chances of an accident. Use your best judgment when in class. It is safer for everyone, including yourself.

Tip 36: Always turn into the barre.

Combinations are always done with the left and right leg in ballet. Once the combination is finished to the right, always turn toward the barre to get to the other side. Every ballet class will turn into the barre. There is a lot of argument regarding why this is done, but it is an unspoken "universal rule." Turning towards the barre to do the other side is something you will always do.

Tip 37: Be ready to start before the music does.

You should be in a starting position, prepared to dance as soon as the combination has been explained. This means standing in the proper foot position and with your arms in the traditional ballet preparation position (en bas). You should return to this same position at the end of your combination. If you had to balance at the end of the combination, return to the starting position, hold still and silently count to 4 in your head before relaxing. All combinations have a start and an end. Returning to this preparation pose indicates that you have completed the combination. It is considered polite and visually indicates that the class is ready for the following combination.

Tip 38: Do not lean, climb, or hang on the barre.

This is directed to little ones who are going to their first class. The barres are made of plastic or solid wood bars attached to the wall. If there are extra portable barres, they are made of metal and incredibly heavy. While the barres look like monkey bars, they are not. Keeping them from hanging or climbing the barres in classes for young ones is a constant battle. If a barre was to collapse or drop away from the wall, your child could be seriously injured.

Etiquette for Center

After all combinations at the barre have finished, dancers then transition to the second part of the class. This second part is dancing in the center of the studio, without the barres for support. Center has a formula that every class will follow. It starts with a slow exercise (called adagio). Adagio requires the dancer to move slowly and gracefully. Adagio involves leg extensions, balancing on one foot, and slow, delicate transitions between steps. These combinations are all about demonstrating your ability to control your body. Adagio combinations involve a lot of strength and focus on not showing how hard you are working when you do it. Ballet is all about making audiences think it is easy and requires zero effort.

After adagio is finished, the class moves on to working on turns. For beginning dancers, this involves introducing pirouettes to students step-by-step. In intermediate and advanced dancers, this involves practicing multiple rotations in a pirouette as well as other types of turns in different positions. The turning portion of the class will start in the middle of the room and may move to the corner. Moving to the corner of the room requires dancers to "perform" turns similarly to how they would on stage, traveling from one part of the floor to another. The final two sections of the class are allégro. In

French, allégro means brisk, lively, or quick. Allegro is divided into two sections: petite allégro and grande allégro.

Petite allégro involves small jumps done in place or moving side to side for a short distance. Dancers work on petite allégro to further "warm-up" for the final portion of the class, grande allégro. Grande allégro means large quick jumps. This is where dancers work on getting a "split" in the air on grand jetes (the big leaps dancers are known for). There are a lot of different kinds of large jumps, and as you advance in ballet, you will learn them.

Tip 39: Personal space.

You need to give yourself enough room to move to dance in the center. When a class is large, the class will be divided into groups of 4-8 people per group. Each group uses the entire room to dance. When you have finished the combination, walk along the sides of the room towards the back. This gives the dancers on the floor from the other group enough room to move, isn't distracting, and is the polite thing to do.

Tip 40: If you don't know the combination, wait and go with the last group.

A combination is usually explained or demonstrated one time before dancers must repeat it with music. Sometimes the combination just doesn't stick in your head. It happens to everyone and can happen in the middle of a combination. You will be moving along fine, and then your brain goes blank. If you are unsure if you have the combination down, place yourself in the last group. This lets you watch the other groups as they dance, and you can see the steps you need to do when your turn comes.

Tip 41: Marking the combination.

In dance, you will hear the word "mark/marking" during class. Marking means doing small movements in place, not using your arms entirely, or using your hands to imitate feet. Marking is not bad; it is how many dancers follow along with the instructor when learning a combination. Some dancers remember combinations 'hen they mark while the teacher is instructing. In the ̲ʋ̲ı, marking is done when practicing a combination before doing it full out or on the sides while other dancers are on the floor.

There is a time and a place to mark the combination; it is when you are learning or reviewing a combination. When it comes time to do the combination with the music in the center marking is not acceptable. All combinations in the center must be done full out.

Tip 42: Behavior for the end of class.

As we have often mentioned in this chapter, respect is important in ballet. This respect lasts until you walk out the studio door. Just as there is a way classes start (at the barre), there is a proper way to end the class. You have to perform the grande reverence, the large curtsy, or bow at the end of a performance. In classes, they are done in a slightly different way than on stage.

When you do a grande reverence, the teacher will usually stand at the front of the room. You will follow the teacher as they do a short slow exercise. What that exercise looks like varies from teacher to teacher but always ends with a curtsy. When the reverence is completed, your instructor will turn to face the class and clap or thank the students for their hard work.

This signifies the end of class and is like the final period in a book. Sometimes there is not enough time left in the class to do a grande reverence. It would be best to approach your teacher and personally thank them for class when that happens. You will walk up to your teacher, do a small curtsy with a slightly bowed head and say, "Thank you."

A reverence at the end of class is also how a teacher shows that they respect you as a dancer. They acknowledge how hard you were working in class, and it is their way of saying goodbye until the next class. Both students and teachers respect each other mutually in ballet, even if it might not seem that way all the time. If there isn't enough time at the end of class for a reverence, it doesn't mean your teacher doesn't respect you. It means that there wasn't enough time in class. That is why dancers and teachers clap at the end of class.

If you are fortunate to have live pianists during class, it is proper to thank them for playing. Not all studios have pianos in them, but I promise you will encounter one during your dance journey. After the grande reverence, your teacher may ask you to turn around and thank the musician. A round of applause is given to the musician, and class ends.

But what if the class didn't end with a grande reverence? Suppose your class does not or did not do a grande reverence. In that case, you should walk up to the piano and do a *small curtsey and thank the musician.*

HowExpert Advice: Always thank the musician before you thank your teacher.

It is important to thank the musicians and be kind to them. The worst thing a ballerina could do is insult or offend the musicians or conductor. There have been professional dancers who were disrespectful to the musicians or conductor. When it came time for the professional to do a solo, the musicians would play faster or slower than in rehearsals as a way to "punish" the dancer. When there is a slight change in your music, it is disorienting and can cause mistakes. This won't happen in class. If you perform with live music, treat them with the same respect you give your teacher. Most conductors or musicians don't do things like that, but it has happened.

Clothing and Hygiene Etiquette

Tip 43: Come to class in the proper clothes.

We discussed what to wear to class in Chapter 2, but it is being discussed again because it is so important. Your child must arrive at class in the proper attire. Proper dance attire is expected for adults, but it doesn't need to be leotard and tights, just loose-fitting clothes for you.

Tip 44: Buy multiple pairs of tights and leotards.

Having fresh and clean leotards and tights is a necessity if your child takes several classes a week. Getting two or three pairs of tights and leotards for classes is wise. Leotards and tights are made with fabric and materials that can't go in the dryer but must be hung to dry. Damp leotards and tights before class starts is not a good feeling, so having multiple pairs of leotards and tights is needed.

Dancewear can be expensive. If you cannot afford the cost of additional leotards and tights, let someone know. You can speak to the director, your child's teacher, or even the secretary and inform them of the situation. Try talking to the staff to get advice on where to find less expensive dancewear. There is bound to be one parent at the studio who has spare leotards and tights their child grew out of at their home. Hand-me-down leotards are a normal thing to see. I bought an old leotard from a guest professional ballet dancer a few years ago. She came to the studio with a giant bag of leotards, dumped them on the floor, and told us to take however many we wanted. Once we found leotards that fit, we gave her, I believe, $5 for each one we found. If you become friendly with parents of dancers who dance with your child, suggest a dancewear swap party. If you can't afford leotards offer to host the event and have a bottle of wine with cheese or something for the parents to enjoy as the kids figure out what fits. My little sister used to get upset because she rarely got to go pick out a new leotard for herself. She would wear ones that no longer fit me.

Tip 45: Throw away any tights with holes in them.

Tights are not made of sturdy materials and can get snagged on anything in the studio or outside. It is common to rip your tights, but you will usually start with a run in the tights.

HowExpert Advice: Use a drop of clear nail polish applied to the top and bottom of the run to stop it from growing larger.

The nail polish trick is super helpful because you can wear tights with runs, but not tights with holes. It is worth tossing a quick-drying clear nail polish bottle in a dance bag if you or your child notices a run. While tights with holes may seem like a minor thing, who cares what they look like as long as your child is wearing tights. Younger children will find a hole in their tights and play with it all class and make the hole much larger than it used to be. Tights with holes look sloppy, and ballet is about looking perfect and polished at all times. If you came to an audition and 20 dancers were auditioning, having a hole in your tights looks unprofessional and can be why you do not pass the audition.

General Etiquette

Tip 46: Listen to your body.

Listening to your body is imperative in life, but even more so in a ballet class. Ballet dancers are told to ignore how they feel and come to class. An old teacher of mine used to say, *"Unless you are sick in the hospital hooked up to wires or dead, you come to class, and you dance no matter what,"* Dancers (especially dancers ages 9 through 18) tend to keep dancing even while injured. The general attitude is that if you can still move or nothing is visibly broken, you can keep dancing. They might not even mention an injury to you, their parent. They honestly might not know if they are injured, as crazy as that sounds. In more advanced levels of ballet, you push your body more and use more muscles, and sometimes it doesn't feel good. Having a sore back/knees/hips/foot is pretty standard, so students will ignore it and assume they are just sore. Ignoring severe pain or trying to return to dance too soon after an injury can lead to surgery or severe injury.

Young dancers who are still growing are more susceptible to injuring their feet. This is because growth spurts are occurring, and they rapidly change the shape and structure of their bones, muscles, and tendons. Stress fractures and knee diseases like Osgood-Schlatter are regular occurrences. Kids have to listen to their bodies and admit when they are hurt, or something doesn't feel right. If your child is injured, take them to a place specializing in sports medicine. Ballet dancers often have the same injuries as people who play contact sports. It isn't good to get hurt, but it happens. It might be a muscle tear, a sprained ankle, or a fracture. An injury is an injury and needs to be taken care of ASAP.

Adults, listening to your body is crucial. Ballet puts your body in positions that are not natural and works all and every muscle in your body. As a result, you will be sore the day after class. However, you know your body and the difference between uncomfortable and injured. If you get hurt during a combination, just move off the side (if you are in the center). Let the teacher know, and they will let you sit and possibly put ice on wherever it hurts for the rest of class.

Please don't let the fear of a possible injury stop you or your child from dancing. Ballet is a sport, and athletes get hurt sometimes. I have had stress fractures, sprained ankles, Osgood-Schlatter disease, broken toes, and other injuries caused by dancing. The number of times I have injured myself outside the studio is far greater than the number of dance-related injuries. Ballet does not fix clumsiness, or at least not for me. However, it has taught me how to care for minor injuries and know when I need to see a doctor or if they will heal on their own.

Tip 47: Accept and apply corrections.

In ballet, your teacher will often correct your positions. Sometimes it is by calling out something like, *"Your arm looks like it is dead," or* physically adjusting your body to the proper position. It may feel like a teacher is picking on you or hates you because they constantly give you corrections. The opposite is true. Corrections are how you get better. If you watch YouTube videos of ballerinas rehearsing a solo with their coach, you will hear the coach talking to them and giving them corrections. The ballerina immediately applies the correction or pauses the music and works on it. I promise your teacher doesn't hate you or think you are a terrible dancer. They just want to see you improve and grow as a dancer. I had a dance teacher who once said, *"Don't worry if you get a million corrections in class. You should be worried when you leave class without a single correction. That means you were average or not worth watching"*. It is a very true statement and is something to remind yourself of after a class where you received a lot of corrections.

When you are given a correction, it is assumed you will apply the correction immediately and remember it in the future. Rolling your eyes or ignoring your teacher and not applying the corrections is inappropriate. It comes across as if you don't care, you think your instructor is wrong, and you know better than they do. Always apply corrections right away.

A great way to improve as a dancer is to listen to the corrections your teacher gives to another dancer and apply them to yourself. Sometimes a teacher makes a correction aloud and doesn't mention anybody's name. In that case, it is directed to the entire class because the teacher sees that everyone could use a reminder. You should apply those kinds of corrections as well. Ballet teachers will give praise too. It is not corrections 24/7; you may be recognized for your hard work in class and during that combination.

Learning to accept and apply corrections can be used outside ballet in places like school or work. Dealing with criticism and truly hearing what the other person is saying makes you a better person to work with or teach at school.

Tip 48: Do not make fun of or laugh at anyone else's body.

If you are an adult dancer, you know by now not to talk negatively about someone else's body. You are an adult and must act like one. This is a tip geared towards tween and teen dancers, who are becoming adults and must act like one as well.

Don't do it. If you hear your friends laughing at someone or mimicking them in an overly exaggerated way, tell them to stop. It is rude and also incredibly mean. In ballet class, your body jiggles, has rolls, you may sweat more than others, or you miserably fail at doing a move. Nobody, not even professionals, looks good all the time. In ballet, your body is moving in unnatural ways, and you will make some strange shapes. There is nothing funny about learning how to do something and not being great at it right away.

The requirement to have a "perfect ballerina body" does not apply anymore. All people care about now is if you are strong and can perform, that has nothing to do with weight. It isn't only making fun of a dancer for being overweight. Bullying in dance studios can be about literally anything, but it hurts in a different way. You have probably been dancing with the same people for years now and are all friends. You may spend more time with the people in your ballet class than you spend with your family in a day. It hurts when someone you thought was your friend bullies you. Some people can ignore what people say, but others can't.

The only time you can laugh at someone's body is if they are laughing at themselves. There are many times when you look ridiculous in classes. Until your body learns how to do a position and the minor adjustments you need to make to do it properly, it's going to look bad. That is the truth and why we take classes, so we look beautiful on stage.

Tip 49: Leave your jewelry at home.

When you come to dance class, you should remove all jewelry. That way, it isn't a distraction and isn't damaged or doesn't cause an accident if snagged. Long earrings or large hoops are a terrible idea for ballet classes, as are necklaces and bracelets. It is permitted for you to wear your engagement ring and wedding ring in class. Nobody expects you to remove them, but you can take them off if it is more comfortable not wearing rings.

Tip 50: Always raise your hand (unless it is a medical emergency).

For younger dancers, you will have to ask for permission and raise your hand to speak as you do at school. Raising your hand means you don't interrupt your teacher when they are speaking. If you have a question wait a few minutes to see if your teacher will talk about the same thing you had a question about.

If you feel sick to your stomach, rushing to the bathroom is fine, emergencies are emergencies. If you feel dizzy, notice if you are not sweating anymore and feel clammy, your vision is getting fuzzy or browning out; you do not need to raise your hand. This means you may or are about to faint. Don't wait until you are called on to let someone know you feel faint. If you feel faint, try to sit down on the floor immediately. Sitting will decrease the likelihood of hitting your head if you do faint. A few times, I have almost fainted or fainted in class. The first time it happened, my teacher noticed I looked really pale and not like I usually do; she was helping me walk to sit down. I took a few steps and fainted. If my teacher hadn't been holding me up, I would have hit my head on the metal foot of a portable barre in the room. I had no clue that I had fainted until I came to, and my teacher and classmates were crowded around me with water and food to eat at the ready. I was around 11 or 12 at the time and noticed that I didn't feel good, but I ignored it and ended up fainting.

Adults, you can raise your hand to ask a question or ask it aloud when the teacher stops talking. You can also quietly leave the bathroom room and know your body enough to know when you are feeling ill or faint. As an adult dancer, you have more freedom than students at any level. That is because everyone in the class is also an adult, and it isn't seen as rude if you have to step out for a second.

Chapter 3 Review

This chapter covered many topics and had a lot of information in it. Some of the biggest things were:

- Being respectful and polite is a must.
- There are two parts of the class, and they have different rules.
  - Turning towards the barre and spacing for the first part of the class
  - In the center, to have personal space, when it is okay to mark during the second part of the class.
- How to properly end each class and thank your musician or teacher.
- To come to class in clothing that does not have holes in it.
- General etiquette for any time you are taking a class.

- Raise your hand if you have a question or need to use the restroom.
  - Adults have more freedom and aren't required to raise their hands.

Chapter 4: Warm-ups and Positions of the Feet and Arms

Warming up is a regular practice in ballet. As we touched on in Chapter 3, ballet classes are taught in a particular order; barre first, then the center. At the barre, the combinations will start with knee bends. Then each subsequent combination will become more complex. While the difficulty will change as barre continues, the muscles and parts of your body used to perform are further warmed up. This allows your body to extend when jumping and not cause injury or lead to a more significant injury. We learned that it is best to come to class early to warm up in the last chapter. In this chapter, we will learn some easy warm-ups you can do before class.

When class starts, dancers are expected to be standing at the barre in a preparatory position. Learning the arms and feet positions will help you feel more confident in your first class. It may be a bit of a surprise, but once you know the six positions of the feet, that is all ballet is composed of. The arms are what is important in ballet. Your arms should help control your body as you move and balance, and it will always be something that you work on in every class.

These are the feet and arm positions you will always use. Your arms will always move between the positions we will learn. Your feet will always pass through these positions. Starting and landing for turns and jumps are the same. The entire time your arms flow between positions. That is all ballet is, making six feet and simple arm positions into art.

Let's begin with our warm-ups!

Tip 51: Begin with seated exercises.

Foot Circles (flexed feet) - for warming up the ankles.

1. Sit with your legs fully extended in front of yourself and have your legs as close together as possible. To start, we will flex the feet; this looks just like if you were standing. Heels on the floor, feet together, toes pointed up to the ceiling.

2. Starting with the right foot, move your foot in a slow circle, keeping your heels glued to the floor.
3. Repeat and do the same thing with the other foot.
   - If you want, you can have both feet in the opposite direction.

HowExpert Advice: Don't skip this exercise.

It might not sound that important, but if your ankles aren't loose and warm, your feet and ankles are bound to cramp once standing in a ballet position.

Foot Rolls – for warming up the feet.

1. Starting in the same position you took for the circles, legs fully extended in front of you, heels glued to the floor.
2. Take your right foot and slowly point the whole foot down to the toes. Imagine you are carefully pushing down the breaks on a car.
3. Do not lift or bend your knees when doing this stretch.
4. Now lift just your toes into a flexed position.
5. And slowly bring your foot back up to the flexed position

HowExpert Advice: Foot rolls can be an alternative to foot circles if you don't have much time to warm up before class.

Butterflies – for opening up the hips.

1. Remain seated on the floor.
2. Pull your legs in towards your body with the soles of your feet touching.
3. Straighten up your spine and press gently on your thighs with your hands. You press your legs down until you feel slight resistance.

HowExpert Advice: If pressing on your thighs gently to move them closer to the ground is painful, you do not need to do it. This option is for dancers to intensify the stretch if they need it.

<u>Splits Right & Left – for opening up the hip flexors and stretching the quads</u>

RIGHT SPLIT

1. Start in a low lunge with your right leg bent and your left leg straight behind you.
2. Move your hands to the side of each hip.
3. Slowly slide or walk the right foot forward until you feel some tension or resistance.
4. Do not move your front foot when you feel resistance or tension behind your knees. Hold the current position and count to 10 in your head.
5. Walk right foot back into the lunge position and stand up (how you stand doesn't matter. The goal is to just return to a natural position without injury.)

- Repeat with the left foot in front for your LEFT SPLIT

HowExpert Advice: Do not rush or force your body into a split. It just places tension in the back of the knee and pressure on the hip joint and muscles.

It takes a lot of time to do a proper split with both legs flat on the floor and your hips squared and pointing forward. It is okay if you cannot do a split, it will happen. One way to help nail your splits is to stretch and do the split exercises every night before bed. For adult dancers, you are never required to do full splits. Just attempting them is enough. The important thing is to listen to your body and not try to force it into a position it isn't used to. It is important to remember that ballet will sometimes feel uncomfortable. Still, you should not be in severe pain and likely to get injured. That rule applies to every person who takes dance classes, regardless of if you are three years old or 83 years old.

Tip 52: Move on to standing warmups.

There are many different kinds of standing warmups you can do. These three warmups suggested are only examples of what you can do.

Lunges at the barre - stretching out calves and thighs.

1. Approach the barres in the room and stand facing the barre. Place both hands on the barre and your feet in a parallel position.
2. Holding the barre with both hands, bend your left knee and slowly walk your right foot backward. You should step back in this position until you feel your calves stretching.
3. Hold that position for 10 seconds or longer it is up to you.
4. Switch feet and repeat.

HowExpert Advice: This exercise is something you can do after a combination has been done on both sides. It is a classic stretch that dancers love. Your teacher may instruct the class to do this exercise.

Foot Trudges - stretches the arch of your feet.

1. Stand with your legs together, facing the barre with your hands resting on the barre in front of you.
2. Bend your right knee until just the ball of your foot is on the ground (a beveled position).
3. Rise onto your tiptoes with both legs, straightening your right knee simultaneously.
4. Bring your feet down to the parallel position, this time keeping the ball of the left foot on the ground.
   • Repeat until you have a steady rhythm, like riding a bike.

HowExpert Advice: If you are wearing pointe shoes, you can do this exercise in two different ways. The first way is just regular trudges to demi-pointe. The second way is to keep your foot pointed with the box on the floor or pressed front in a deeper arch.

Parallel leg swings – to loosen the hips for lifted leg exercises later in the class.

1. Place your left hand on the barre and stand with both feet pointing forward.
2. Place your right hand on your hip, lift your right leg up with a bent knee and swing it from the front to the back of your

body. If doing this exercise in attitude, remember to hold your leg in a proper attitude at 45 or 90 degrees.
3. Swing your leg back and forth 16 times and then turn around, place your right hand on the barre, and repeat.

HowExpert Advice: Your upper body will pitch forward and backward slightly when your leg swings. It is naturally going to do that. If you are moving your upper body from the force of the swings, engage your abs and stand with a long spine to reduce the excessive movement in the upper body.

Standing Quadriceps stretch – for stretching your quadriceps.

1. Stand facing the barre with your feet parallel and your left hand resting on the barre.
2. Lift your right leg with a bent knee and grab hold of your ankle/toes/foot with your right hand.
3. Slowly straighten your body, keeping your knees touching and bringing your foot up to your rear end.
   * Repeat on the other leg

HowExpert Advice: This isn't a new or ballet-specific stretch, but it's nice because the quadriceps are activated or extended for almost all barre. Plus, the stretch feels good.

Stretches and warming up before class help prevent pulled, strained, or torn muscles. Like an Olympic runner who stretches and warms up their body to prepare for a race, dancers do the same for class and performances.

The Six Ballet Positions for Feet

Every step done in ballet will begin from, move through, and end in one of the six positions in every combination. When you think of ballet like that, it sounds simple and can help you learn new steps by seeing what positions the feet move through.

You could stand up and do a "ballet position" with both feet on the floor; everyone is familiar with the positions. At first, these positions will feel weird, which is expected. Standing with each foot pointed in a different direction with straight legs or rotating the legs into the proper position is awkward at the beginning. I promise these will become muscle memory by your third or fourth class.

Before we jump into the ballet feet positions, we need to talk about what makes the positions feel challenging to stand in. Turnout. Turnout is your new best friend. You will not get through a ballet class without the word "turnout" said less than 20 times. In ballet, your leg will be rotated in your hip socket outwards. To stand in the six positions, turnout and engaging specific muscles are needed.

Ballet is full of metaphors to help dancers visualize new positions. Using the mirrors is helpful for learning the positions of the legs and arms. I will be using a lot of metaphors in this section and the one following. It may sound like something you say when teaching a child. Hopefully, it works and will help you remember what the positions should look like.

Tip 53: First Position.

In First Position, you must stand tall and have your heels touching and your toes pointing to the sides. Your feet should be flat on the floor, and the arches of your feet shouldn't roll forward. Standing with your legs completely straight is the goal. An excellent way to discover your natural turnout in First is to rock back on your heels. Then open your feet like you would open a book in the middle. Put your feet back on the floor in this position, and that is how far your turnout is. Everyone has different amounts of turnout their body can allow. Forcing turnout leads to bent knees, and straightening them puts your legs over-rotated position.

When you stand in First Position, your feet and having straight legs are not all you have to think about, there is a lot more than just the feet. The entire body must be engaged. This means your feet are in First Position with heels touching; legs are touching and rotating outward, and your knees are not facing the front. Your hips will be facing the direction you are standing. Your derrière (French for back/behind/rear) will be squeezed and tucked under your hips.

This means that your derrière and lower spine are not in a swayback position. When I teach little dancers, I tell them this about squeezing their derrière:

"Let's pretend we have a grape in our hand. We will take that grape and put it between your butt cheeks. Now when we stand in our Positions, I want you to squeeze your bums so tight to make the grape becomes grape juice."

It is silly, and the kids think it's hilarious. But after telling them this and occasionally saying, "Are you making grape juice?" every child will engage their derrière muscles right away. This would align their pelvis and lower spine to the position it needs to be in. For adult dancers, this grape story feels a bit juvenile. But, trust me; if you imagine making grape juice, you will squeeze your derrière, which allows you to fully engage your turnout.

Tip 54: Second Position.

If you have First Position down, Second is a breeze! Start in First Position and then slide your feet apart, so your heels are no longer touching. Like in First, your toes will be pointed to the sides with your heels down and turned out. In Second Position, it is important to make your second wide enough that you can bend your knees easily in that position, but not too wide.

For Second Position, think of a dog house. When you are in second and do a demi plié (slight knee bend), your legs should look a bit like a dog house if you look in the mirror. Your thighs are the roof, and the space the dog would go into starts from your knees and to your toes. If your Second Position is too small, the dog can't fit; if it is too big, the roof will be too big and will fall down.

You should not feel any strain on your knees and ankles. If you do, make your second position a bit smaller by stepping your feet closer together. Your teacher will likely tell you to make your Second smaller or larger. This is to make sure your feet are in the proper position.

Tip 55: Third Position (and when you will use it).

Third Position is like the second cousin twice removed when it comes to feet positions. This is because it is old-fashioned and has primarily been retired in the ballet world. Unless it is at the barre, it is good to learn Third Position because it is similar to Fifth Position. I know that makes no sense, and just in case you take a class at a studio. They say they want "pliés in Third" you will know what your feet should look like. When this guide was written, I had been dancing for 24 years, and I had never been asked to do Third Position.

For Third Position, stand in First Position. Slide your heel of one foot to touch the arch of your back foot. Your feet will still be turned out, and your thighs will start to cross slightly. If you look down in Third Position, the space between your back heel and toes of the front foot will be at a 45-degree angle. If the position is uncomfortable or your feet start to cramp, move the ball of the front foot to a wider angle.

Adult dancers and dancers returning to ballet classes (after two or more years) may feel their feet cramp in the arch. This means your Third or Fifth Position is too tight. If you start cramping, your position is too tight and can lead to injury.

Tip 56: Fourth Position.

Unlike Third Position, Fourth Position is used a lot. Fourth Position is how a pirouette begins. Having a solid understanding of Fourth Position helps when you start learning pirouettes. Fourth Position is similar to Third, but your feet will be further apart. Starting from Third Position, slide your front foot forward about twelve inches. Distribute your weight equally on each foot.

Weight distribution helps you stay upright in Fourth Position. Remember to engage your derrière (grape juice). In Fourth Position, your feet may remind you of duck feet which is good. Your Fourth needs to be crossed enough but not too crossed. This means making sure your feet are aligned, and your hips are square to the front. The alignment of your feet in Fourth should be that you can draw a straight line from the heel of your front foot to the heel of the back leg. If you have ever seen a tightrope walker standing on a rope, their feet are pointed out, like Fourth Position.

Tip 57: Fifth Position.

Fifth Position is the most challenging position and can do a number on your knees if it is done improperly. Fifth Position is a tighter Third Position. Where your heels and toes meet on each foot changes in Fifth. You will see that shifting from Third to Fifth is a breeze. Remember to stand up straight, engage your derrière and keep your legs straight. That will help you keep your balance.

To do your Fifth Position, stand in Third Position (the heel of the front foot is touching the arch of the back foot). From your Third Position, slide your front leg over until your rear toe touches the heel of your front foot. It may be challenging, but it becomes more manageable. By your second or third class, your Fifth will be correct.

It is important to know how to do Fifth Position. When I teach younger/pre-ballet level students Fifth Position, I tell them, *"Mr. Toe kisses Mrs. Heel."* It is an easier way to picture Fifth Position in your mind and can make sure your Fifth is crossed enough. Then, when you move into the center, every combination will start in either First or Fifth Position.

Tip 58: Sixth Position.

Technically, there is no Sixth Position. Yet it is a position you will use more frequently than you will use Third Position. Sand with your feet together, so your feet are parallel to your body. That is it. That is Sixth Position. If you have a combination at the barre and your teacher says, "Okay, starting from Sixth...," you will know what that looks like.

Basic Positions of the Arms

Time for a ballet history lesson! Ballet methods can't agree on what the arm positions should look like or what they should be called. There are five methods of ballet, and you will usually dance in one style or a combination of a few. (I will be referring to each method by its "first name" for simplicity)

The first method is The Cecchetti Method of Ballet (pronounced like Cha-Ket- Tea). You will hear it called "Cecchetti" or "Italian Method/Style" method. This style is a ballet training method created by the Italian ballet master Enrico Cecchetti. His method was based on anatomy and learning to dance by understanding how each part of the body works and moves. A student will only learn new movements in this method once others are perfected. In a training school that uses Cecchetti, you move up levels by passing a "performance assessment." This assessment is on steps and positions learned in that level and the prior levels. In this method, quality is more important than anything else. Why bother with movements if you do them incorrectly when you can do them correctly every time.

The second method is The Vaganova Method. You will hear this being called "Vaganova," "Russian Style," and "The Soviet Method." Calling this technique style Soviet is outdated (the method wasn't created in the Soviet Era). It was developed by Russian ballet dancer/master Agrippina Vaganova. This method is totally different from the Cecchetti Method. In Vaganova style training, there is an emphasis on several other elements of ballet. Vaganova teaches that a dancer's arms (port de bras) should be expressive. Not just things you robotically move. The arms move with the body and should help the dancer with longer turns and higher jumps and leaps. Flexibility, more specifically extreme flexibility, is a large part of the style. Vaganova believed that the lower back needed to be both flexible and strong. If that wasn't enough, ballet is seen as an endurance sport. It requires the same amount of energy and detail at the start of class as and at the end when your body is tired.

The most prestigious ballet training school is The Vaganova Academy in Saint Petersburg, Russia. Some dancers who graduated from the academy include Anna Pavlova, Svetlana Zakharova, Rudolf Nureyev, and Mikhail Baryshnikov. Search Vaganova Academy Exams/Graduation Exam on YouTube if you have the time. Watch to see how dancers are expected to move.

The third method of ballet technique is The French Technique. This may be referred to as "French Style," but it's rare. The French method dates back to the 17th century and has been the foundation of all the other styles. This method focuses on moving between steps and positions fluidly, creating clean and seemingly effortless lines. Beyond that, the emphasis on the épaulement was stressed. Épaulement means "shouldering" and describes the movement and location of the shoulders and head. No épaulement is beyond boring to watch because it is stiff. This method is prevalent, and the following two methods borrow from this method. Ballet originated in France, and this method is typically taught in studios with a mix of the following method.

The fourth method of ballet is The Bournonville Method, sometimes called the "Danish Style." Created by August Bournonville, this style is strongly influenced by the French method. Both styles use graceful épaulement and the eyes moving with the head and body. This casts the illusion that the dancer is dancing with zero effort. All styles focus on "making it look easy" and making audiences think you are a wisp gliding gracefully across the floor.

What differs from the French method in the Bournonville method is quick movements of the feet compared to other methods. Vaganova is like dancing in a swimming pool, slow and controlled. There is a variation in the leg position while doing whipped turns, such as fouetté turns. Everyone knows or at least has seen fouettés being performed. They are the turn where the dancer turns on one foot and the other is bending at the knee and opening the slide each time. Beyond a pirouette, this is what most non-dancers will imitate if you ask them to show you "ballerina turns."

The final style is England's Royal Academy of Dance (R.A.D) Method. Everyone just calls it R.A.D. R.A.D is an academic approach to ballet training. There are ten levels; students have to start at Level 1 and pass a board-certified performance exam to move to the next level. R.A.D is centered around the idea that basic techniques and steps should be learned slowly to learn more difficult steps faster. This method is a blend of the four previous styles.

Unless a studio specifies their method, you will likely learn a blend of French and Bournonville methods. Still, other styles may be added as well. I learned a "style" that is a blend of French, Bournonville, and Vaganova methods. There is no right or wrong method, and one is not better than the other. Each method is ever so slightly different.

With that being said, we can move to the basic arm positions. In each position, I will label it with the names I use when I teach and include the terms used by the other five styles. Some positions have different names, and it can be confusing but learning the shapes is an excellent place to start.

Tip 59: en Bas.

Pronounced as "on baa," this is the position your arms will start with when at the barre. Put your arms in front of you and pretend you are holding a giant beach ball against your chest to do this position. Your elbows will be rounded, and your hands have a few inches left before the touch. Once you have your beach ball arms, hold that position and lower it down to your hips. Your arms will not touch your body and will rest slightly outward. It is important to stand tall and keep your shoulder location in mind. Shoulders are always pressed down; even when your arms are up, your shoulders are pressed down.

Names for this position for each method:

- Bournonville - Bras Bas
- Cecchetti - Fifth en Bas
- French - De Départ, Preparation Position, Au Repos, or Première en Bas
- Vaganova - Prepratory Position
- R.A.D - Bras Bas

First Position in Cecchetti and Bournonville methods looks like the en Bas position we just learned. Except you open your arms a bit wider, to the outside of your hips. It gets a bit confusing because Bournonville and the Cecchetti methods are different from First Position arms in the other three methods. Note the names that those two methods call what everyone else knows as First Position.

The other First Position is just raising your en Bas position up until your middle fingers would touch your sternum if you pull the arms in. You can also think of holding a beach ball up to your chest. You don't want your arms up too high because you can't see over the ball. On the other hand, you don't want them so low that it looks like you can't decide if you're going to do First Position or stay in en Bas. You did a combination of both. The elbows are always tricky at first because you aren't used to them being held in such a way. It is essential that your elbow is making your arms curve, not straight out to the side for all the arm positions. You don't want your arms to look like what an old teacher of mine used to say, chicken wings. If your arms are not far from your body and curved, your arms look exactly like a chicken wing.

Names for this position for each method:

- Bournonville - Bras Arrondis Devant (Devant is French for "before'), or First Position en Avant (en Avant is French for "in front of").
- Cecchetti - Fifth Position en Avant
- French - First Position
- Vaganova - First Position
- R.A.D - First Position

Tip 61: Second Position.

Second Position is the easiest but also the one that requires constant awareness. Hold your arms out to either side and bend slightly at the elbow to create a soft curve. If someone were to come and try to push your arms down, they shouldn't be able to force your arms down. Press your shoulders down and engage your latissimus dorsi muscles (lats) to control the body.

Your lats work the entire time you dance. They are the muscles that connect your arms to your body at the back. The lats help stabilize your spine and provide shoulder strength to your body. In dance, you should imagine there is a piece of string that runs from one lat muscle to the other. To engage your lats, envision someone pulling down that string in the middle. Your lats will drop and be held in place. If you have ever seen Swan Lake, the swans don't flap their wings from the elbow. It is all in the lats and shoulders to give a soft, delicate flowing motion.

The elbows should never bend more than a slight curve that you have done en Bas and with First Position. It is easy to let your second droop. When you dance, you think about many things, and it is common not to think about the arms. As a result, the elbows will start to droop. Utilize the mirrors in the room to see if you have chicken wings. You can check the mirror while you dance and fix anything that looks wrong. That is why there are so many long mirrors in the studios. Just turn your head slightly when at the bar and glance at your position in the mirror.

Names for this position for each method:

- Bournonville - Bras à le Linge, or Second Position
- Cecchetti - Second Position
- French - Second Position
- Vaganova - Second Position
- R.A.D - Second Position

I have never had an instructor call Second Position anything besides Second Position. Bournonville's alternative name is included if you go to a studio or a class that uses the Bournonville method.

Tips 62 & 63: Third Position & Fourth Position.

Third Position is combined with Fourth Position because some ballet methods call the arm shapes different things. Some methods do not recognize certain positions as a "real position," and the shape of the arm positions varies. We are going to start with Third Position.

Third Position is one of those arm positions that all of the methods of ballet can't seem to agree on. Some separate it by one of the arms is not raised and the other way the arm is raised. It sounds confusing, but the explanation below will make it a bit clearer. Ballet may be largely universal, but a few positions and names are very different.

For this position, we will start with the low arm style. Place your arms in First Position and open only one arm to Second Position. The other arm stays in front of your body. Still remembering to keep the lats engaged and your shoulders pressed down.

Names of the low arm style Third Position for each method:

- Bournonville - Third Position Low
- Cecchetti - Fourth Position en Avant
- French - Third Position?
  - The French method does not recognize this as an official position
- Vaganova - Small Pose
- R.A.D - Third Position

In the second version, the raised arm style is easy to get to from the low position. Lift the arm in the front upwards. You want to look out for droopy wrists (zombie's wrists). If you were to stand in this position and look straight up, you could see the raised arm. If you can't see the arm, your arm is too far back and needs to be brought forward.

Names of raised arm style 3rd position for each method:

- Bournonville - Third Position en Haut (en Haut means "at the top")
- Cecchetti - Fourth Position en Haut
- French - Third Position?
- Vaganova - Big Pose
- R.A.D - Fourth Position

Moving on to Fourth Position arms. You can move straight from Third Position en Haut by curving the arm out to the side in front of you.

If you are asked to do this position, it will be during the slow leg extension combinations in the center (adagio). When used in combinations, the teacher is more likely to demonstrate this arm position when teaching it.

Names for this position for each method that uses Fourth Position One arm up, the other curved in front of the body:

- Bournonville - Fourth Position
- French - Fourth Position
- R.A.D - Fourth Position Crossed

In my experience, I can't think of a time when Fourth Position was ever said by a teacher anywhere else besides the center. When in the center doing the adagio, I heard one of three phrases used:

- "When moving from the promenade, take your time to bring that arm behind you for the arabesque."
- "Let's start/finish with your arms in fourth."
- "Right/ Left arm up."

The best thing to do is watch the teacher demonstrate and hear what they say as they demonstrate. If you have the wrong arms, your teacher will loudly say your name and "wrong arms." Your teacher will only mention it in any level of adult classes if you have the wrong arms. It is normal to put your arms in fourth when doing arabesques, but that fourth is entirely different.

If you are a boy and take a men's class, you will do more Third and Fourth Position arms because they are in most choreography for men. Turning with the arms in Third or Fourth Position, ending on one knee at the end of a solo, and pretty much all the time.

Third and Fourth Positions arms are seen in many Spanish-based ballets or Spanish characters for both male and female dancers. Some examples would be:

- Solos and the grand pas classique portion of Paquita
- Esmerelda Variation
- The Spanish dance from The Nutcracker
- The Spanish dance from Swan Lake
- Don Quixote

Tip 64: *Fifth en Haut.*

Fifth en Haut is one of the classic ballet arm positions. If a teacher says just en Haut, then it will be this position for your arms that they want to see. This position is straightforward to get to. Put your hands above your head as you did in raised Third Position and Fourth Position, except use both arms. Remembering your posture, engaging all your muscles, and being aware of your hands and elbows continues even in this position.

In a proper Fifth en Haut, your arms will not be in a straight line down to the shoulders. Instead, the arms are angled slightly forward, and your middle fingers should be in line with your forehead. If your arms are too far behind you, it changes your center of gravity, making balancing and turning challenging. It also is uncomfortable. It ratchets your shoulders behind you, and your chest will push forward into a very open position. Even if you are a beginner, you will be able to tell something isn't quite right if your Fifth en Haut is too far behind you.

Names for this position for each method:

- Bournonville - Á la Couronne or Fifth Position
- Cecchetti - Fifth en Haut
- French - Fifth Position or Bras en Couronne
- Vaganova - Third Position
- R.A.D - Fifth Position.

Chapter 4 Review

- Three basic seated warm-up exercises
- Three basic standing warm-up exercises

- Ballet feet positions First to Sixth
- Different schools or methods of ballet
- Ballet arm positions
  - The other names you may hear in class

Chapter 5: For the Adult Beginner — Advice from an Adult Dancer

I have met so many people who have said things to me like, *"I used to dance ballet when I was little but stopped. I wish I could take classes now,"* or *"I am too old to start learning ballet."* It is sad to hear this because it is not something that will prevent you from learning ballet. More likely, they are too afraid of being embarrassed. You will have an embarrassing moment or several moments in a ballet class, which is okay. However, learning from those embarrassing and awkward moments will make you a better dancer. It happens to everyone.

When I was 18, I was rehearsing a solo on stage, and my foot slid out from under me, and I fell. I fell incredibly hard, and the sound of me hitting the floor was comically loud. The sound crew stopped the music because they thought I was injured. Then, I hear my little sister yelling from the stage's wings to make it more embarrassing, "ARE YOU DEAD? BECAUSE YOU ARE MY RIDE HOME".

A friend of mine, who is now a professional ballet dancer, slid on some fake snow during the Nutcracker. She slid off the ballet flooring and onto the very slick black wood at the front of the stage (known as a blanket). She ended up sliding and falling off the stage. She got up, put on a big smile, and finished the dance at the ground level in front of the first row of the audience. When she came backstage at intermission, she was so embarrassed. After the show, all the audience could talk about was how professionally my friend acted in that situation. How amazed they were that she fell off the stage and got back up once she had her bearings and smiled like it never happened.

The embarrassing moments happen, but the only way to move past them is to smile/laugh at yourself and keep dancing. Sometimes gravity gets the best of you, but everyone else in the class has experienced it too. So now it is time to get past feeling embarrassed and move forward. As an adult dancer, I want to share some advice for you, the adult beginner.

Tip 65: You are never too "old" to start ballet.

When I say age doesn't matter, I mean it. I have taken classes with adult dancers who were so many different ages. While taking classes at San Francisco Ballet, there was an 86-year-old woman who came to class with pointe shoes on. Adult dance classes from beginner to advanced levels are full of women and men who tried ballet, liked it, and kept taking classes. I've been the youngest dancer in the room many times. I've had a middle-aged woman approach me asking if I was lost or wanted to borrow her phone to call my mom to come to pick me up because it was an adult class. I was wearing pink tights and a bun to an adult class, and I was mistaken for a teenager... I was 24 years old. Nobody cares how old you are or look in an adult class; ballet has no age limit. You aren't too old to start if an 86-year-old woman can take a two-hour ballet class in pointe shoes.

Tip 66: Showing up at your first class is something to be proud of.

Starting ballet as an adult makes you incredibly brave. Not because it has the slight potential to be dangerous, but because you did what many adults never do. Show up for the class. I have met adults who have mentioned they wanted to take a class and signed up or even paid in advance to take the class. However, when the day of their first class came, they never showed up. They said they wanted to do it but were so afraid of looking bad or dumb that they decided not even to try.

It is common to be nervous when you start something or go somewhere new. I've been dancing for over two decades, and I still get nervous when taking my first few classes at a new studio. That is normal, but pushing past those nerves and coming to the studio and finding a spot at the barre to stand is an incredible accomplishment.

Tip 67: Don't be too hard on yourself.

There is a reason professionals dedicate their entire lives and all their time to dance. It took them years to get to where they are now. Ask any professional dancer if they were good starting out, and they will all laugh and tell you they were awful. That is because everyone learning something brand new isn't immediately amazing at it. In ballet, you have to let the small things go. Or try using that mistake to find the motivation to back to class to try it again. You are making your body do things it has never done. So be kind to yourself and not beat yourself up if something goes wrong.

Tip 68: Your height, weight, or fitness level does not matter.

Say it with me, "*my height, weight, and fitness level do not matter.*" This idea is something I hear all the time, even before I was an adult. There are short ballerinas and tall ballerinas; I am one of the taller dancers. Nobody will tell you that you are too short or tall to start ballet classes. If someone does, find a better studio. It does not matter if you have had seven kids, are heavier than you want to be, or are normal-sized. You are not a professional, and your shape or size does not matter. You can be missing limbs and still take classes (a bit of modification and creativity is all you need).

"*I'm not in shape enough for that.*" This is the most frustrating excuse people give for why they haven't tried or won't sign up for a class. To be honest, not a single dancer of any gender identity thinks they are in shape enough and everyone starting new physical activity isn't in shape right away. Coming to classes is a way to improve how fit you are. Ballet requires strength, stamina, balance, and energy, so you will get more in shape by dancing.

The problem that many people have is that they have a warped vision of what they should look like in order to do even a single step of ballet. Yes, in the past, the ballet world has put a lot of emphasis on being as thin as possible. However, this idea is changing because now the value is placed on solid dancers who can have much energy. Being incredibly underweight puts stress on your heart, your bones become brittle, and your body will get tired before class ends. In an adult beginner or any adult dance class, you aren't expected to have the body of a professional dancer.

Tip 69: Your flexibility will only improve as you take classes.

Nobody will ask you to immediately drop into a split as soon as you find a place at the barre. Flexibility is something that improves through stretching at home and working hard in class. Barre is structured to warm up your body, so you will have the ability to be more flexible for center work. It is okay if you can't get your leg up to your head. You don't have to do that. Trying to make slight improvements from class to class or lift your leg a bit higher this week is what matters. If you want to improve your flexibility, stretching for an hour or so before work and before bed can help. Never force flexibility because it can lead to torn muscles if you push your body too far.

I had to take a 2-year break due to an injury, ballet studios were closed due to the COVID-19 pandemic, and I lost a lot of my flexibility. My first class back in a studio was in January of 2022, and it was rough. I didn't understand why; I had been dancing all my life. Now suddenly, I am getting cramps in my feet, back, and legs? What is wrong? What was wrong was that I was trying to dance like I was 18 and dancing every day again. Flexibility is a slow process, but it will get better. It is just something we all need to get into a habit of regularly doing.

Tip 70: Everyone in class is focused on themselves, not you.

This applies to teens and adults who are just taking classes recreationally. In class, you are more focused on using every muscle in your body, and so is everyone else. The only person watching you is the teacher. They watch everyone dancing to see what the entire class is struggling with and correct positions that are wrong. You don't need to worry about other people in class watching and judging you. As an adult dancer now, I am only focused on what I am doing and how my body feels. When I take a peek at the mirror to see if it looks like I am doing things correctly, I am only looking at myself, and so are all the other dancers.

In a large or small class, it is easy to see all the mirrors in the room and feel like everyone is watching you. However, if anyone is watching you, it is because they forgot the combination and are looking at you to know what to do next. Even then, they aren't judging how high your leg is in the air; they are trying to catch up with the rest of the class.

Tip 71: It is impossible to be perfect.

I had a dance teacher tell a class I was in when I was around 13 years old:

"If you think you are perfect and can't find a single thing to fix, improve, or work on, it is time to quit dancing."

Ballet always strives for perfection, but it is impossible to be perfect. You can do a combination well with no mistakes, but you can always do more. For example, use your head and eyes more, point your feet, or stand straighter. Even professionals who look flawless on stage will have a laundry list of things they could have done better when they get off the stage, such as more turns, a more sustained balance, and being on time with the music. If you feel like you are perfect and there is nothing to improve, ballet is not for you. The inability to be perfect and wanting to be better than they were last class is what motivates a dancer. As an adult beginner, don't stress about trying to be perfect. Only try to be a little bit better than the last class. Enjoy the class and let yourself have fun without the pressure of perfection.

Tip 72: Don't worry if your first few classes are overwhelming and you feel a bit lost.

Feeling lost or overwhelmed is a normal part of starting ballet. Remember that you are being taught French words for positions and steps. You have to move your body into positions it is not used to and remember combinations. It is a lot. I promise the overwhelming feeling you may experience in the first few classes will go away as you continue to take classes.

Tip 73: Any teacher who will not slow down or help you isn't a good teacher. Find a new studio or a different class.

You will come across teachers who are stunning dancers, but they are terrible at teaching. Your teacher should slow down or help if you ask for it for any beginning-level classes you take. You can say things like, *"Can you repeat that a bit slower?"* or *"Can you help me?" "I don't know that position/I forgot what that step was,"* and things like that. If your teacher ignores you or doesn't try to explain and show what they are doing, they don't care about teaching. Teaching beginning children is a lot different than teaching beginning adults. Some teachers are just better at working with kids and try to teach an adult class in the same way. If you feel like your teacher is not helping you understand what to do, it is okay to find a different class to take. It can be with another instructor, or you can find a new studio to attend.

Tip 74: Just try it.

As an adult beginner, you may have moments when you think, *"my body does NOT work that way."* (Again, ballet is unnatural and feels strange at times.) The only way to learn and improve is to try it. You will be surprised at how much your body is capable of achieving. If you have been attempting and physically are unable to do something, try doing it slower or smaller. Ballet is a lot of trial and error, and trying steps or trying for more turns is the only way you can get better and advance.

Tip 75: Tell your instructor if you have an injury or an old injury that acts up.

Re-injuring yourself or making an injury worse is what we try to avoid in ballet. As an adult beginner, letting the teacher know you may not be able to do a particular step is essential. Ballet can always be modified, and there are many alternative ways to do a step. For example, I developed a tumor on a nerve in my right foot in college. I know certain things will hurt to do if constantly repeated. I informed my current dance instructor of the condition and that I may not be able to do some things. I was told to dance until it became too painful and then change the combination to my comfort level.

That is the proper response for an adult dancer. Teachers for adult classes are adults themselves. If they were former professionals, they would have pain in their bodies as well. They understand that an injury can be more severe and take longer to heal when you are older. Please don't be too shy when it comes to injuries or extreme discomfort. This isn't *Dance Moms*; nobody will be mad at you if you have to change the combination slightly.

Tip 76: Bring a small notepad or notebook in your dance bag for corrections.

It is a great idea to keep a notepad or notebook and a pen in your dance bag. After class, you should write down at least one correction you received. It doesn't matter how to spell the steps; this notebook is for you only. Before class, you can read over the corrections in your book to remember things to work on.

Tip 77: You do not have to go en pointe. Nobody expects you to do pointe work.

This was mentioned earlier, but students will take a pre-pointe class to do pointe work. These classes are designed to strengthen their feet and ankles. If you want to dance with pointe shoes, I recommend talking to your teacher before or after class about it. They can tell you if it is possible for you to do pointe and what needs to be done before a shoe is on your foot.

If you just want to dance and the shoe doesn't matter, perfect. Adult dance classes are about you and what you feel comfortable wearing or doing. You may see women in your class who are wearing pointe shoes. This is because they danced when they were younger and kept taking classes in pointe shoes. People will wear pointe shoes in class just to keep their feet and body in "pointe shape" by dancing in them. I've done class in soft shoes and pointe shoes in the same week. Nobody said a word besides a woman who also wears pointe shoes joking that now she has to work in class because she is alone in pointe shoes.

Whatever you do, do not go and buy yourself a pair of pointe shoes! It doesn't matter if you are professionally fitted for the shoes or did some late-night shopping on Discount Dance's website and got yourself a pair. I cannot stress this enough, don't do it. Your feet and ankles aren't ready, and your house doesn't have a ballet studio floor. Pointe shoes on anything except a studio floor (or concrete for photo purposes) is like standing on a rolling chair at work to grab something off a shelf, an accident waiting to happen. Many adults don't do this, but a few here and there are so happy to finally be able to take ballet classes that they want to look "like a ballerina."

Tip 78: If you mess up or find yourself going in the wrong direction or using the wrong leg, don't walk off or stop.

In ballet, you never just stop in the middle of something and stand there lost or leave the stage. From a young age, dancers are told to quickly look at the person next to them. Whatever that person is doing, do it too. Usually, by then, you aren't lost or remembered the choreography. It is easier to use the mirror to see what you are doing wrong in class. All you need to do is take a breath and fix the mistake. At some point, you will end up on the wrong leg or completely forget the combination. It is okay, but it's best to catch up or correct yourself as soon as you notice that what you are doing is not what the rest of the class is doing.

Tip 79: You are going to be sore after your first class.

Ballet uses every muscle in your body. In class, you may notice your legs are shaking at times. You may be feeling stiff a few hours after you finish the class. You will definitely be very sore the next day and for a few days after. Your legs are shaking because the muscles are working incredibly hard, and it is something just to ignore; you are okay. Icy Hot and Epsom salt can help relieve the soreness. You shouldn't be worried about it, you haven't injured yourself, and any discomfort will disappear. Taking class regularly will prevent being constantly sore. If you have to miss a few weeks, your first class back will leave you sore.

Tip 80: Other adults are dancers, and there are tons of blogs, chat rooms, and social media pages. That is an excellent way to meet other adult dancers.

Sites like Facebook and Reddit are great places to join a digital adult dancer community. These are places where you can ask for advice and tips and just chat about ballet. Everyone there loves dancing and loves talking about it. Sometimes it can be hard to make friends in an adult class, but digital forums can help you connect with other adult dancers.

Tip 81: Don't wear a leotard if you don't want to wear one.

Comfort and mobility are all that matter in adult dance classes. Many of the women I danced with when this book was written wore black leotards and pink tights. I am used to wearing a leotard and tights, so I wear them when I dance now. For me, leotards are comfortable, and wearing one makes me feel prepared to dance. I can't go to class if I am not wearing a leotard. It makes me feel like I'm doing something bad... I'm not, but 24 years of strict ballet training tends to stick around. Honestly, in every adult ballet class, former dancers and new ones will wear a leotard and tights. There are also former dancers and beginning dancers that will never come to class in a leotard; they don't want to. Some wear a mix of both. Wear what you want, except jeans.

Tip 82: Leave all your problems outside the studio doors.

To quote Joel Grey as the Emcee in the classic musical Cabaret;

"Leave your troubles outside! So - life is disappointing? Forget it! We have no troubles here! Here life is beautiful...."

Life might not always be a cabaret, but one place you should always leave problems outside is at a ballet studio. When you are in a class, that is all that matters; you must be present physically and mentally. It is an hour or so of your day where you don't have to worry about anything. Just have fun and dance. Ballet (or dance of any style) can be good for you mentally. Ballet won't cure you, but it can help stop obsessive, intrusive thoughts and anxiety for an hour. In addition, taking a ballet class after work can help many adults transition from work mode to relaxation mode.

You can spare an hour or hour and a half just to ground yourself, even on the busiest days.

Tip 83: Not sure if you will like the class? Don't buy dance clothes until you know that you like class.

Dancewear can be expensive for adults. You don't need to buy leotards or ballet shoes right away if you sign up for class as an adult. Wearing a thicker pair of socks works, as well as wearing ballet shoes in class. If you want to buy all the dance gear you want, that is great! Just know that you are not expected to do so.

Tip 84: Everyone has a bad ballet day.

You will have classes where you can't balance or feel like you are doing everything wrong. Having a lousy ballet day is more common than you may think. Reminding yourself that it is normal to feel so frustrated that you want to quit at times can help you feel better. Ballet isn't about perfection. It is about constant improvement.

Everyone feels that they look bad when they see themselves dance in a mirror. However, ballet master and co-founder of the New York City Ballet, George Balanchine, said it best "_The mirror is not you. The mirror is you looking at yourself._" So be gentle to yourself and remember ballet is for fun even if you are working towards being a professional.

Tip 85: Try at least three classes before you quit.

Before deciding that you do not like ballet or dancing, take at least three classes. After three classes and you still hate it, quit. Sometimes the first class you take can be different than you thought it would be. It is okay if you don't like it but taking three classes allows you to decide if you genuinely do not like ballet.

This is a recommendation I give anyone trying to learn something new for the first time, especially the performing arts. I will always encourage anyone who wants to take a ballet class, but I know it isn't something everyone will love. Watching ballet in a theater is very different from physically being in a class working at the barre. Ballet is difficult and takes many years to get "good at it," You must keep that in mind when starting classes.

Tip 86: If you are a man and slightly interested in seeing what ballet is like, come to class!

Ballet is for men, too; society has labeled the arts incredibly feminine, but it is not the case. Nobody in a dance studio in an adult class will think less of you or think you are not "masculine" enough. Plus, a little boy waiting for his sister to get out of class will see you and make him interested in dance too. Finally, ballet class is a terrific workout, and you won't need to go to the gym if you go to ballet class.

Chapter 5 Review

- Some advice from an adult dancer to adult beginner dancers.
- You are never too old to start, and showing up to that first class makes you brave to try something new.
- You will never be perfect, so don't worry about not being amazing right away. It takes time and hard work, and the goal is just to be better than you were last time.
- Wear what makes you feel comfortable, and you do not have to go en pointe.

- A studio is a place to leave your troubles outside the door and can be therapeutic for some dancers.
- Everyone has a bad ballet day. Try to take at least three classes before deciding not to take classes anymore.

Chapter 6: All About Pointe Shoes

Since they were first developed, pointe shoes have been part of the magic of ballet. If I mention I am a dancer, the most frequent question I am asked is, *"Do you have pointe shoes/dance on your toes?"*. Pointe shoes and how they allow dancers to stand on their toes are always interesting for non-dancers and young dancers. Besides a tutu, pointe shoes are the most identifiable feature of a ballet dancer.

Pointe shoes are things that are both complicated and simple. There are many brands and models of shoes to choose from. Every dancer has a different way of preparing their shoes for class and the stage.

A Brief History of Pointe Shoes

In 1795, French dancer Charles Didelot wanted the female dancers in his ballet company to look light enough that their feet hardly touched the floor. He created "The Flying Machine" for dancers to wear under their costumes. The Flying Machine used wires to lift the dancer higher when they jumped or as they glided across the stage.

While audiences thought it was unique, the wires were visible and bulky. Costumes had to be built around the wires and harnesses. As a result, all ballet companies did not widely adopt the Flying Machine.

Early 19th-century ballet dancer Marie Taglioni was the first dancer to dance on the tips of her toes without wires. Audiences were amazed and wanted to see her dance. Marie was and still is a significant character in the history of ballet in Europe. She was one of the most famous ballerinas of the "romantic era" of dance. The shoes Marie Taglioni created were silk shoes with thick leather soles, and the toes and sides were darned to keep the shape of her foot. Other ballet companies began to require their dancers to wear similar shoes. Unfortunately, these early pointe shoes were incredibly uncomfortable. Dancers would rely on foot and ankle strength alone to stand on the tips of their toes.

During the late 19th century, Italy began making pointe shoes that were an improvement on the shoes created by Marie Taglioni. These new shoes had a flat, sturdy platform at the front ends of the shoes. This flat platform created a solid surface that dancers could balance on. Before now, nails were used to attach the thick sole to the shoes. The nail in the center of the shoe provided a tiny bit of support. The nail was removed with the Italian pointe shoes, which made the shoe silent, and only the toe area was made stiff.

In the 20th century, Russian Prima Ballerina Anna Pavlova developed a more "modern pointe shoe." She put very firm leather soles in her shoes and flattened the toe area of the shoes. Once the shoes were flattened, she would harden them to create a small box-like shoe. She found that the box-like shape gave her more support than the other two iterations of the shoes. Until Anna Pavlova, the toe shape and structure of pointe shoes were soft on the side, with the firm areas located at the sole and tips of the shoes. Originally this material at the tip of the shoe was made of wood or layers of burlap glued together and dried. That is where the "pointe shoes are made of wood" belief comes from.

Pointe shoes continued to evolve as time went on until they became the shoes we use today. In the 21st century, some pointe shoe soles are made with plastic. In addition, there are now pointe shoes in various shades of brown to match dancers of color. Light pink was used traditionally because it matched all the dancer's skin because they were all white dancers.

Tip 87: The anatomy of a pointe shoe.

A pointe shoe is made of five components:

The Box - stiff toe tip with a flat surface to stand on. Usually made of many layers of paper, burlap, and cloth glued together and shaped on a foot-shaped mold. When the glue dries, it makes the fabric hard.

The Vamp - part of the shoe that runs from the top of the box/platform to the opening of the shoe.

The Wings - the sides of the shoe.

The Shank - a rigid material that makes up the sole of the shoe. They are usually attached to the inside and bottom of the shoe with 1 or 2 small tacks. Materials for shanks depend on the brand of shoes. Typical shank materials are layers of leather, cardstock, flexible plastic, and burlap. They are layered and glued until hard.

Ribbons and Elastics - the shoes do not come with the ribbons and elastics attached. A dancer has to sew them on, and it can take up to two hours to attach them securely.

Tip 88: Breaking in the pointe shoes.

The shoes are very firm and flat when the ribbons and elastics are sewn on. This is because every dancer's feet are different, and the shoes are not customized; the dancer has to customize them to their liking. To help the shoe follow the dancer's foot's shape and feel comfortable, all dancers "break in" their shoes. Each dancer likes to prepare their shoes differently, and the ways to break the shoes in can get a little crazy.

The first method is to put the heel of the shoe in a door and pull the box towards themselves as they slam the door closed. This causes the glue in the shank to break and makes them less rigid.

The second method is to beat the vamp and box of the shoe on the walls, floors, stairs, concrete, or any sturdy surface. This is done to make the vamp and box softer. This also is done to make the shoes less noisy when landing jumps. Some people like soft boxes to help make their feet look more arched.

The third is to cut out half of the shank inside the shoe (or rip it out) and remove the first tack. For dancers with flat feet ripping out the shank inside the shoe is very common. Removing part of the inside sole and the tack means the shoes are more flexible at the arch. In addition, three-quarter shank shoes come with shorter shanks, so a dancer doesn't have to cut and remove the shanks themselves.

The fourth method is to crush the vamp. The top of the foot curves slightly when the foot is pointed; crushing the vamps makes it bend with the shape of the dancer's foot. This is typically done by placing the vamp under the heel of your foot and forcefully pressing down the weight of the body into the heel. The vamp will make a crunch or cracking sound and flatten out a bit. Some professional dancers have been known to pick up curtain weights backstage and drop them on the shoe (while not wearing the shoe).

The fifth method is to stick the side of the vamp into a water fountain or apply rubbing alcohol to the shoe area that needs to be softened. The water or alcohol softens the layers of glue, and the dancer can better shape it to accommodate the front of the foot.

Some dancers only do one method others do all the above and more. You can break in your shoes by taking a class or two in them, but it is easier to break them before you wear them in class. When I break in new pointe shoes, I step on the vamp with my heel. That is all I like to do, and then I will take classes in them to find that it works best for me and my feet. When I started pointe, I tried the other methods, but they didn't offer me the support I needed. There is no right or wrong way to break in pointe shoes, and the shoes naturally break in the more they are used. Anything goes as long as the shoes are not too soft or the shank is too low to support the foot.

Tip 89: Hardening the pointe shoes.

Some dancers with flexible and strong feet need to make their shoes harder. There are three common ways dancers can harden their shoes: shellac, glue, or baking the shoes.

The first method for making pointe shoes harder is to apply shellac to them. A dancer will paint the inside of their shoes (box and vamp area) with shellac (the kind that is a varnish on wooden floors). Once the shellac is applied, they leave them to dry for 24-48 hours before use. The shellac hardens as it dries, making the shoe more sweatproof. Heat and moisture from sweat cause the glue in the shoe to break down, and the shoes will be unusable; shellac helps to delay that process. The shellac always goes inside the shoe and never on the satin or bottom shank of the shoe.

The second method uses super glue to coat the area where you need more support. A product known as "Jet Glue "is explicitly made for pointe shoes. Jet Glue can be purchased at most dancewear/dance shoe stores or online. Both kinds of glue make the shoe stiffer, and usually, only a small amount is needed. Unlike the shellac, which is applied all over, super glue or Jet Glue can be applied near the wings or shank of the shoe. This is done to extend the hardness further than the shoes are or on the shank inside or outside the shoe. I like to use Jet Glue and apply it in a square in the middle of the inner and outer shanks. This is because I have broken the tacks in the shoe, or the shank has become too soft and is unable to distribute my weight properly. Also, hardening shoes makes them last a bit longer, which I need because buying 4-5 pairs of shoes every month was incredibly expensive.

The third method is to use floor wax and bake the shoes in the oven. To do this, preheat an oven to 200 degrees Fahrenheit. While the oven is warming up, use a paintbrush to apply the floor wax inside the shoe where they need extra support. Once the oven is preheated, turn the oven off and place their shoes into the oven. The shoes are left overnight in the oven with the door open, and that is it. The wax and baking method is done because once the wax hardens, it becomes a layer of firm plastic.

Not all dancers need to harden their shoes. I didn't harden my shoes for the first year or two of pointe and only started to because my teacher recommended I try. Even though hardening the shoes can make them last longer, every pair of pointe shoes dies at some point.

Tip 90: Dead pointe shoes.

"Dead" shoes are what dancers call pointe shoes once they are worn out. This can take several months or only a few classes. Many professional ballet dancers will wear out their new pointe shoes in one performance. Once the shoes are dead, they need to be replaced.

Shoes will all die because the heat and sweat of your feet break down the layers of glue and makes the shoe softer and less supportive. Along with moisture absorption, the pressure placed on the shoes makes them die. When on pointe, the amount of pressure on the shoes is four times the dancer's body weight. Pointe shoes can break in different places for each dancer.

Boxes can die or become too soft to dance on. When this happens, your foot is not in the proper position, and the distribution of weight will shift. When the box dies, it will typically be in one area of the box rather than the entire box. Press all over the box with a finger to test if your box is broken. If the shoe dimples under your finger when you press on it, they are dead. A broken box can cause arthritis, bone spurs, and sprains. The shoe will buckle under the dancer's body weight and can result in falling. It can also cause the shoe to buckle when the dancer tries to step en pointe. It will throw them out of alignment, causing injury almost instantly.

The shank of the shoes can also die. The shank will crack, or the tack holding the shanks together can be bent out of shape or snap completely. When a shank breaks, the shoe is less sturdy and cannot properly hold the dancer on their boxes. A broken shank forces the dancer's entire weight on the top of the foot. The dead shank shifts the dancer's center of gravity. You usually will be able to feel when the shank dies, but if you can't, there is a way to test it. Hold the shoes by the heel in your fist and wiggle them. If the shank is dead, the shoe will be floppy. Pointe shoes are supposed to be stiff, and a dead shank can lead to stress fractures in the bone in the feet and ankles, sprains, and bruising of the foot bones.

If you continue to dance with dead shoes and do not replace them puts you at risk of tendonitis, bursitis, and torn tendons in the feet and ankles.

Tip 91: Lifespan of pointe shoes.

Brand new, fresh from the factory, pointe shoes have an average life span of anywhere between 10 and 20 hours of use. That is it. Not a long lifespan, and the more you dance, the more the shoe breaks down. All pointe shoes will die and need to be replaced eventually.

Tip 92: They hurt, but there are cushions for your toes.

Any ballet dancer who says pointe work doesn't hurt their feet is lying. They hurt professionals and beginners. While you get used to the pain, wearing the shoes for several hours becomes uncomfortable. When a dancer goes from standing flat to standing on the top of the box, the feet sink into the shoe slightly. The inside of the shoe is very hard, and when your foot moves in the shoe, it will rub against the rough material and cause blisters. Bruised toenails are common for those wearing pointe shoes. The skin on your feet will develop calluses which are ideal, but if you wear pointe shoes, you will get water and blood blisters at least once. Corns and bunions are common, and many dancers get them removed for comfort. Some dance teachers tell students to soak their feet in methylated spirits (or denatured alcohol) for a few hours a day to toughen up the skin.

There are cushions that can make pointe shoes less painful. They do not relieve or prevent the pain, but they make wearing the shoes easier. The toe cushions dancers use varies, and it is okay to try different products if you don't like the one you use now. Some dancers do not like any protection at all. The most important thing with cushions is to use enough to still be able to feel the floor underneath you. There are several different products dancers use as cushions in their shoes:

Taping Toes

Some dancers like to tape their toes before putting on their shoes. Wrapping toes with tape helps prevent blisters from getting worse and can prevent blisters. Band-Aids work but the medical tape sticks to sweaty toes better. A single toe can be wrapped in tape, or several toes can be taped together. Taping the toes together is a way to support toes by limiting the ability of the toe to move.

Gel Pouches (name brand "Ouch Pouches" also referred to as toe pads)

ch is a thin layer of gel or Styrofoam that is placed
two pieces of fabric. There are also gel toe caps. These are
,-like tubes with gel inside them that can either go on the
, or other toes. A dancer will trim the stocking to make a
beanie for the toes. It sounds silly, but they look strange and are a
little cap for your toes. The gel pouches and toe caps protect the
toes from blisters and can make the big toe less painful.

Lamb's Wool

Lamb's wool has been used in pointe shoes for many centuries. A
dancer takes loose wool and wraps it around the foot to make a
slight nest shape for their toes to rest inside the shoe. Many dance
studios tell kids to use lamb's wool, but many people do not like to
use wool. I used it when I first started wearing pointe shoes, but I
hated how it felt. It made my toes incredibly sweaty and didn't
protect my toes from rubbing the inside of the shoe to prevent
blisters. Lambs' wool used to be the only thing dancers would use in
their shoes. Wool is thin enough for the dancer to feel the floor
under their feet.

Paper Towels or Tissues

For paper towels, the dancer will put their toes in the middle of the
towel and fold and wrap the rest of it around their foot. The goal is
to make a pocket shape around the foot. It is almost the same for
tissues, but some people use several sheets of tissue instead of just
one.

You can cushion your feet however you want, but if the material is
too thick, you won't be able to feel the floor. It can also cut off
circulation and make the shoes too small.

I like to use a gel toe cap on my big toe and either a gel pouch or
tissues in my shoe. I like to use tissues only during performances
because I use three tissues for each foot, which can be wasteful. I
put the pouch over my feet and pull the tights over my foot to hold
it in place.

Tip 93: Am I ready for pointe?

This was mentioned in Chapter 1, but there is a lot of debate about the age at which dancers start pointe work. In the United States, most studios wait until a student is 12 or 13 years old before beginning pointe. Waiting until 12 and 13 is recommended by doctors because the foot has finished growing by then. As a child, the bones in the foot are shifting. The growth plates fuse together, become harder, and the bones tend to stop growing during puberty. If you fracture a growth plate before the foot is done growing, it can cause permanent damage. Eleven years old is edging toward being too soon for pointe, but it happens often. The Youth American Grand Prix added a rule that strongly discouraged competitors under the age of 12 from wearing pointe shoes. Pointe shoes are prohibited for dancers 11 years old and younger and can lead to disqualification.

Dancers in Russian Method schools and the Vaganova Academy in Russia will start at ten years old. This is normal and to be expected. The reason students under 12 start pointe is because the students have to audition and are selected on their physiques. Flexibility, height, how good their feet are, etc. Once they are accepted, the students train extensively every day. The type of feet the dancer has and the constant training strengthen the Russian Method dancer's feet faster.

Age isn't the only thing teachers consider when assessing their students to determine readiness for pointe. Maturity is a significant factor as well. Pointe shoes are slippery and are dangerous if the shoes aren't worn or used correctly. A more mature dancer is less likely to play in their shoes. Playing in your pointe shoes would be not using proper technique and attempting skills that the dancer has not done in flat shoes first. The strength of the ankles and feet is so important when it comes to starting pointe work.

While pointe shoes are sturdy and have a platform and tip made for being danced on, those features do not matter without strength. There are two ways dancers shift from flat feet to en pointe. One way is a relevé which involves bending the knees and using the floor to push up and onto the shoes. The other way is an elevé which uses the strength of the feet and ankles to lift the dancer to the tips of the shoes. Dancers need to be able to do both relevé and elevé without holding onto the barre, which requires a bit more strength to achieve. Strong feet and ankles are required when only standing on one foot and balancing. The entire weight of the body is balanced on the tip of the shoe. Being able to hold yourself up and not injuring your foot takes strength in the ankles. In the end, it is up to the ballet teacher to determine if someone is ready for pointe.

Tip 94: Get fitted for your shoes.

Do not buy the first few pairs of pointe shoes online! The sizing of the shoe is different from soft shoes and street shoes. Someone needs to fit you in your first few pairs of shoes. Staff at dance stores are trained to fit a dancer with pointe shoes. They will have you try several shoes and narrow down the brand and model of shoes. If you can, ask the dance teacher where the best place to buy the shoes from or whom to make a fitting appointment with if you can see if the teacher will go with you to try them on so they can make recommendations to whoever is fitting you.

Your teacher may recommend or require everyone to start in the same make and model of shoes. My class was told to ask for Bloch Aspiration pointe shoes and any other Bloch shoes if those didn't work. I wore the Aspirations for my first three or four pairs of shoes, but I did not like the shape of my foot in that pointe shoe. I then asked to try different kinds of shoes. Today I wear either the Russian shoe company Grishko, and the model is their 2007 with an H or SH (hard or super hard) shank. These feel sturdier in the box area, and the support of the shank is good for when I am doing hops en pointe. Dancers often have to jump and land en pointe or hop en pointe in many ballets. I also wear Gaynor Minden pointe shoes. I can customize them to have narrow width and the hardest shank they make. These shoes use flexible plastic shanks, which means the shank can't die like my shoes usually do. Instead, the toe material deteriorating is why and when it's time to buy new shoes. You can stay with one model and one brand only or try others. The shoe fitting is the most important thing.

Chapter 6 Review

- The history and development of pointe shoes.
- The anatomy of the pointe shoes.
  - Box, Vamp, Wings, Shank, Ribbons, and Elastics.
- The ways dancers break in their pointe shoes.
- How to harden pointe shoes.
- Dead shoes and what that means.
- The shoes hurt, but there are many ways to cushion the toes when wearing pointe shoes.
- 12 to 13 years old is typically when a dancer is ready for pointe.
- Have a professional fit you for your first few pairs of shoes.

Chapter 7: Boys Dance Too!

"Ballet is for girls!"

This belief that only girls and women can be ballet dancers is something the dance world has been trying to change for so long. One major reason is that male dancers are mocked even to this day. The most recent example of this stereotyping and mocking was in 2019. Laura Spencer, a news anchor, mocked England's Prince George on national television. Mrs. Spencer laughed when learning that the young prince would be taking ballet classes at his school. An activity he chose for himself. Likewise, a grown woman laughed at a 6-year-old boy who decided to take ballet classes at school.

The response of the dance world was instantaneous. 300+ dancers took a ballet class in Time Square. Lengthy posts and videos posted on social media about men and boys dancing. Many professional dancers were angry. Because even in 2019, boys were mocked for taking dance classes. The idea that dancing or learning ballet is feminizing and boys who dance will grow up to be weak is incorrect.

Why do professional sports players take classes if ballet is so bad and something to be ashamed of? The NFL has been known to have dancers on its staff for cross-training. These dancers work to improve players' agility. Helping with flexibility, balance, faster reactions with their bodies, and footwork. If professional football players take ballet classes, ballet must not be "too girly." So many young boys and even adults are discouraged by society from ballet which is a shame.

Tip 95: *Men have been ballet dancers since the Renaissance.*

Men have been performing in ballets alongside women since the 1500s. Upper-class people and royalty in those times would learn to dance and perform in the royal court. These performances served as entertainment at banquets and special events, like coronations. A male ballet dancer you have never learned about was King Louis XIV of France! King Louis XIV was known to be incredibly passionate about the art of dance. One of his court musicians and choreographer would cast the King in the ballets he created.

The most noteworthy performance King Louis XIV starred in was a ballet in 1653 called Ballet de la Nuit. The king was only 14 at the time but was cast in five roles in this incredibly lengthy 12-hour ballet. King Louis danced in the role of Apollo, God of the Sun, and after that performance, Louis XIV was known as The Sun King. The king founded what is now known today as The Paris Opera and Ballet Company. King Louis XIV only stopped dancing due to many illnesses, obesity, and gout.

Today, male dancers will have roles that require immense strength and stamina to perform. For example, male dancers will have to execute technically difficult solos. Another major aspect of ballet for male dancers is having to dance with the female dancers in the company.

Dancing with a female dancer is known as partnering. Partnering is when the male dancer holds, carries, lifts, and supports the female ballet dancer as she dances. The complicated lifts in ballet need male dancers to have strong arms and legs. One of the most challenging ballets for male dancers when partnering is Romeo and Juliet. Romeo dances with the body of Juliet, whom he believes is dead. The dancer in the role of Juliet must rely on Romeo to hold her up and move her while acting lifeless and limp.

Even though ballet often looks effortless, partnering is challenging, and carrying a body that isn't moving while dancing and acting is exhausting. What adds to the challenge of this scene of Romeo and Juliet is that this moment occurs near the end of the ballet. By the time Romeo must dance with a dead Juliet, the male dancer has been performing for around two hours. Lifting 100+ pound weights for two hours without rest would be challenging, even for bodybuilders.

Even if you are not a dancer or have never seen a ballet, you know or have heard of two male dancers. These men are some of the most well-known male ballet dancers in history. Russian dancers Rudolf Nureyev and Mikhail Baryshnikov. These men were masculine, loved ballet, and helped shape the history of ballet in the 20th century.

Tip 96: Boys have a better chance of becoming professional dancers than girls.

Men are highly valued for their strength and stamina in ballet. To become a professional dancer, each person has to audition for a contract to join a company. In these auditions, there are noticeably more women than men. Standing out in a large group audition increases your chances of being hired by a company. When everyone in the room is talented and dances well, it is easy for judges to start to feel like everyone blends in. This is true for female ballet dancers; they all begin to look the same in a large audition room start. For men, it is the polar opposite. The men will be more noticeable in a room with 50 women and only three or four men.

This is not to say that male dancers do not need to be incredibly talented. They must be strong, great at turns and jumps, and have excellent musicality. Becoming a professional ballet dancer requires you to be almost flawless. Male dancers do not get a free pass to join any company in the world they want to. Men are not given a contract at the end of every audition for being a man. All ballet dancers must work hard to be professionals. It is important to be realistic and aware that a male dancer is more likely to become a professional than a female.

Things to Know for the Parents of a Future Boy Ballet Dancer

Tip 97: All studios have a spot at the barre for boys.

Studios may be painted pink and have tiaras around as decoration, but they are spaces for boys and girls. Almost all studios have a male and a female or single gender-neutral bathroom. There will never be a time when your son will be exposed to girls and vice versa. Depending on how large the studio is and how many boys there are, there may be a men's dressing room/lounge. They are just like female dressing rooms/ lounges. They have a bathroom or some stalls, a couch, and an area for the dancer to put their belongings during class.

When I was a kid, the first studio I attended had a bathroom/lounge for the boys and a separate one for girls. The middle school and high school boys would use the space. The younger boys didn't use the room as much because their parents typically would wait at the studio for them to finish a class. As mentioned earlier in this book, ballet is about respect. Respect for each other's space, belongings, and privacy. If a boy or girl is hanging out in the other's dressing rooms, being asked to step out while someone was changing was a rule to be followed immediately. Dancers become very close friends over years of dancing with the same people. Respect trumps friendships every time, regardless of gender.

Boys and girls will take classes together. A dance teacher does not have to overhaul how they teach because a boy is in class. The fundamental techniques for ballet are the same regardless of gender. There is no differentiation between male and female techniques in the first eight or so years. When the girls start pointe work, they may have a class separated by gender. Men do not need to learn pointe, many do for fun and strength, but it isn't a part of the dance curriculum for boys. Due to that, there will be a "Men's Class" that the boys will all take together.

Tip 98: What are Men's Classes?

For studios that offer Men's Classes, these are classes led by a male dance instructor for male students. The class is all about teaching the boys steps that women do not do in ballet. Male dancers have many steps and jumps that women are not taught how to do. These classes also involve exercises like crunches, push-ups, working on turns, and jumps. Working with a male dance instructor gives the boys the best training and advice on performing complex steps. This is because the instructor was once or may currently be a professional ballet dancer.

Not all studios have enough students or male instructors for a Men's Class. However, that is not an issue. While the girls are working on pointe exercises, the teacher will alter combinations for the male student. The goal of a Men's Class is to prepare the boys to rejoin the girls for partnering classes. Partnering is a large part of ballet, and both the girls and boys should learn it. In a partnering class, the boys and girls dance together. They will learn how to do different things like lifts and turns. One of the first things covered in partnering classes is an assisted pirouette. An assisted pirouette in ballet is when a man stands behind the woman with his hands on her hips or waist and spins her around a few more times in a pirouette.

Sounds easy, right? It is hard but the best way to start. The boys will learn to stand in the proper position to prevent both dancers from falling. The boys will then practice placing their hands on the girl's hips and keep her balanced on their shoes. The men can feel when their partner is off balance and can move their arms a bit to correct the balance. Then the turning part. It is scary for both boys and girls to do this turn from start to finish. The girls are told to fully trust that their partner will catch them and not hesitate. They must then turn and pull their arms in so their partner doesn't get hit. The boys are told that they do not let their partner fall whatever happens and know when to grab hold of their partner and spin them a few more times.

Sometimes parents do not want their child to participate in partnering classes because it involves touching someone else. While some partnering moves may seem like something sexual, I promise the opposite is true. Both dancers are sweating profusely, likely frustrated with their partner, and focused on what they are doing. Doing something inappropriate is the farthest thing from their minds. Most of the kids are scared to hold each other's hand... nothing inappropriate happens in most partnering classes. Ballet is not a sexual sport in any way, shape, or form, which brings us to the next topic I dislike having to talk about.

Tip 99: *Being a ballet dancer will not make your child a homosexual.*

This idea of ballet is used to keep boys away and ignore interest in learning to dance. I had a dad yell at me for turning or trying to turn his 4-year-old boy into a homosexual because I was teaching the class how to skip. This little boy started class by kissing every girl on their hands because *"a prince in a movie did it, and I am a prince."* Yet skipping made him, a 4-year-old child, a homosexual? This happens all the time and discourages boys from taking ballet classes or makes them quit even if they love to dance.

There are gay male ballet dancers, but there are also gay female dancers. I danced with a gay male dancer who said that going to ballet and hanging out with girls all day made him feel comfortable. Nobody saw him as a threat or weird for being slightly more feminine than other guys at the studio. He said the ballet community was one of the few places he felt he could be his true self and is the reason he did not try to commit suicide a second time. A parent should want their child to have a space just to be themselves; who cares if it is in ballet classes. Ballet is not sexual, and if your child comes out later in their life, it has nothing to do with ballet. Boys, do not wear tutus unless it is for fun but never on stage. Tutus are for women. Men typically wear tights and either no shirt or a tunic. In ballet, the men are made to dress like men.

Tip 100: *The amount of makeup a male dancer wears is less than you think.*

Anyone performing on a stage has to wear makeup. The stage lights wash you out, and your features blur together. Ballet has acting in it, and being able to see the facial expressions while seated in the audience is essential. Male actors on stage and on television wear more makeup than male dancers. The makeup isn't for class. It is just for a performance.

Makeup for Male Dancers

- *Foundation or powder*
  - To even out the color of the skin and cover any blemishes or 5 o'clock shadows for older boys.
- *Blush*
  - The stage lights make a face look featureless, and blush is used to add definition to the face.
- *Eyeliner*
  - To accentuate the eyes.
    - Different than women's eyeliner. It is typically just a diagonal line that angles up from the outer corner of the eye.
- *Lipstick*
  - This may not be needed; if it is required it isn't the bright red color female dancers use, men will mostly use a nude shade.

Tip 101: Wigs are not worn all the time.

Both males and females will have to wear a wig or fake hair at some point in their lives. The wigs are worn to make a dancer fit with the time and character they are playing. Many ballets took place in the 1500s and 1600s, where men wore white powdered wigs while in the castles or as noblemen. Wearing period-accurate costumes is how ballets tell the story visually. Both men and women may have to wear a wig in these ballets, but it is only for the performance. Boys won't be asked to wear a wig in class unless it is brand new and the dance teacher wants to see how he looks wearing it. When there aren't any boys at the studio, girls have to dress up like boys or men with short wigs and fake facial hair. Girls will have to wear wigs and fake curly hair over their bun in many ballets. For both boys and girls, wigs are only a costume and are only worn for a very short time during a performance.

Tip 102: Boys dress like men and play male characters.

In ballet, the male dancers are always dancing in male roles and are dressed like men. There are a few exceptions, but they aren't common; we will discuss them soon. Usually, in any ballet, the male principal dancer or male dancers will be portraying masculine characters like:

- *Kings*
- *Pharos*
- *Sultans*
- *Princes*
- *The man in the village that all the girls want to marry*
- *Soldiers*
  - *Greek*
  - *Roman*
  - *Toy Soldiers*
- *The main love interest*
- *Greek and Roman Gods*
- *Dracula*
- *Dr. Frankenstein and/or the monster*
- *The Prodigal Son*
- *Hunters*
- *Knights*
- *Romantic characters from classic books*

The exception to the "male dancers play male characters" rule is for some character dancers. Character dancers are typically male dancers or former dancers who will dress up as the bad guy in the ballet. Masks or makeup, and usually a cape, is part of the typical character dancer's costume. Character dancers sometimes need to be men because the costumes are often too heavy for a female dancer to dance or walk while wearing them. For example, the Mother Ginger character has children pop out of her skirt in the Nutcracker. To fit all the children under the dress, it is incredibly wide and made of metal. A man has to be attached to a brace and frame, and then the costume is put over those. This character's costume can weigh anywhere from 60 to 150 pounds.

Another instance when a man will have to be a female character is in Sleeping Beauty. A man usually plays the role of the evil/wicked fairy. They do not have wings but are covered in black and green cloth. This character often does very little dancing but does run around the stage bent over, acting mysteriously. When the fairy disguises herself as an old hag, who brings the spindle that pricks

Princess Aurora's finger to put her to sleep, it is a man too. They either wear a mask of an old woman's face or have special effects makeup applied to make them look like an old hag.

In some versions of Cinderella, the mean stepsisters may be male dancers. They will even wear pointe shoes and too much makeup. This is done to make the sisters look ugly, look visibly larger and taller than Cinderella, and is done for comedic effect. The sisters dance badly, make crazy facial expressions, and fall over onto the floor. They act dramatically because the characters are supposed to be laughed at.

Girls will have to be male characters at many studios where there aren't any boy dancers. This was touched on in the last tip, but wearing a short wig isn't the only way a girl must play a role of a boy. One ballet where girls dress as boys is the Nutcracker. For instance, the boys at the Christmas party at the start of the ballet are girls. They wear pants, vests, caps, and very minimal makeup, while the girls wear dresses, have bows in their hair, and have lipstick on. The Nutcracker prince's army of toy soldiers is sometimes only girls that are tall enough to wear the costume. The Rat King's rats that attack Clara are also girls (you can't see the dancer's face under big rat masks). There may be one or two boys in these groups, but sometimes dancers have to play the role of the opposite gender.

I would be remiss if I didn't take a moment to talk more about the subject of dancers playing opposite gendered characters a bit more. This is not done to make fun of or make a dancer feel uncomfortable with their identity. Wearing a wig and being silly as a girl character if you are a boy shouldn't feel wrong or bad. It is a role in a performance—a character. You are still your same gender identity in a costume as you are when you are not wearing the costume. For any dancers who identify as transgender or nonbinary, if playing a boy or girl character makes you uncomfortable and triggers dysphoria, let your teacher know. It is ballet; it is for fun and should not be traumatic, involve bullying, or will cause anxiety about a character or going to class. If a teacher bullies you for your identity, leave that studio and never return. In the arts, gender identity, sexuality, or anything else, doesn't matter.

All that matters in the arts is if you have talent or something you like to do for fun.

Parents still worried that their child dancing with a trans or nonbinary dancer will make them "become trans" should pause a moment. Identity isn't like the flu; it isn't contagious. Dancing with trans or nonbinary dancers is not bad, and if you are worried about this for your child, I have good news. You aren't the person who is taking the class! Let your child decide if they want to start ballet or stop ballet, even if they are very young. If your child tells you they are uncomfortable or scared of dancing with a dancer who is a different gender identity, disabled, or non-neurotypical, then consider quitting classes. Dancers come to class and work hard because they want to be there, not because they are forced to be there.

Tip 103: Boys might be able to take classes for free.

Some dance studios that want to have male dancers and keep the ones they have from going to another studio will charge reduced tuition for boys. Studios may waive the tuition entirely and let your son come and take as many dance classes as he wants for free. Not all studios do this. If you search for local ballet studios suitable for boys, you will likely find at least one studio offering discount rates for male students. Many full-time dance schools, training programs, and summer intensives award full scholarships to boys who want to attend a summer intensive and/or professional ballet school.

There is one final thing to mention for boys who are in or want to start ballet classes. Unfortunately, kids in school may tease your child when they find out they are a ballet dancer. Remind your child that those kids are dumb and don't know just how much of a workout each class is. If they love dancing, being teased shouldn't stop them from being happy and having fun. If any teasing happens, it will likely be in elementary or middle school when kids are still young. Your child can tell people he does ballet or choose not to mention it but remind him that he doesn't have to keep something he likes to do a secret. Boys have a very bright future in ballet and other dance forms; we don't want that future to dim.

Chapter 7 Review

- Men have been a part of ballet since the 16th century, and even today, they can be professional male dancers.
- Men have a better chance of being professional ballet dancers than women.
- Boys and Men of all ages are always welcome in a ballet class and deserve a spot at the barre.
- There are special classes for boys to learn male dance moves and work on lifting and partnering with the girls.
- Ballet will not make anyone homosexual. Ballet isn't sexual.
- Boys sometimes wear makeup and wigs. But, most of the time, they are dancing as masculine male characters.
- Dance studios treasure the male students and may give discounted tuition or free classes for a male dancer.

Conclusion

Ballet makes strong, determined, respectful, and passionate people from an early age. A dancer doesn't quit if they can't do something or do it correctly. Instead, a dancer will repeatedly practice until they can do it and go back to perfecting it by practicing. It is important to understand that ballet is complex, exhausting, and frustrating at times. Yet ballet is also beautiful, fun, and exciting. It is a great way to exercise and an art form that should surround each individual with a loving and passionate environment.

Ballet has made me the person I am today, but it has also helped me emotionally. I have terrible anxiety and depression and have had them since I was a child. When I am stressed, taking even one dance class helps me feel less anxious. It gives me space away from a desk or couch where I can focus on dancing instead of how many projects I need to do. Taking an hour or an hour and a half for myself where I can mentally and physically relax is very healthy. Plus, I always feel really good while coming home after class. I could have been terrible and messed up the whole time, but at the end of the day, it doesn't matter. You get the same endorphins from ballet that you get from a workout class or the gym.

Don't let anything stop you if you want to learn how to dance ballet. You can find a class anywhere or remotely. Adult dancers should attend classes in person for a few months to get used to proper positions. After that, all dancers can take dance classes online through videos or remotely participate in live classes using programs like Zoom or Skype. These recorded classes can be a way to take a class more than once or twice a week. The best tip anyone can give you about starting ballet at any age is to take a class. If you don't start taking ballet classes, you will never know if you like ballet. Or, you won't be able to make a childhood dream come true. You will never experience how hard in love you will fall with this style of dance. A book can only teach you so much, so get out there, find a studio and have fun!

About the Author

Lauren Dillon is a multifaceted writer who has been dancing classical ballet for over two decades. She has worked as a dance instructor for children and enjoys sharing classical ballet with others. Born and raised in Florida, Lauren was inspired to take ballet classes by her mother, who took ballet classes as an adult. Lauren earned her Bachelor of Arts in Russian & Eastern European Studies from Florida State University (FSU). After moving across the country to California, Lauren earned her Master of Arts in Museum Studies from the University of San Francisco. When she wasn't visiting museums or working in a performing arts archive, she continued to dance at San Francisco Ballet and Alonzo King LINES Ballet.

HowExpert publishes quick 'how to' guides on all topics from A to Z by everyday experts. Visit HowExpert.com to learn more.

Recommended Resources

- HowExpert.com – Quick 'How To' Guides on All Topics from A to Z by Everyday Experts.
- HowExpert.com/free – Free HowExpert Email Newsletter.
- HowExpert.com/books – HowExpert Books
- HowExpert.com/courses – HowExpert Courses
- HowExpert.com/clothing – HowExpert Clothing
- HowExpert.com/membership – HowExpert Membership Site
- HowExpert.com/affiliates – HowExpert Affiliate Program
- HowExpert.com/jobs – HowExpert Jobs
- HowExpert.com/writers – Write About Your #1 Passion/Knowledge/Expertise & Become a HowExpert Author.
- HowExpert.com/resources – Additional HowExpert Recommended Resources
- YouTube.com/HowExpert – Subscribe to HowExpert YouTube.
- Instagram.com/HowExpert – Follow HowExpert on Instagram.
- Facebook.com/HowExpert – Follow HowExpert on Facebook.
- TikTok.com/@HowExpert – Follow HowExpert on TikTok.

Printed in Great Britain
by Amazon

10832630R00062